Reading

with the

Troubled Reader

Margaret Yatsevitch Phinney

HEINEMANN
Portsmouth, NH

HEINEMANN
A division of Reed Elsevier, Inc.
361 Hanover Street, Portsmouth, NH 03801-3912
Offices and agents throughout the world

Cover photo©Gabe Palmer/Masterfile.

Library of Congress Cataloguing-in-Publication Data

Phinney, Margaret Yatsevitch.

Reading with the troubled reader.

Bibliography: p.
Includes index.

1. Reading – Remedial teaching.   2. Reading disability.
I. Title.

LB1050.5.P48 1988   372.4'3   88-11211
ISBN   0-435-08480-1

10   Printed and bound in Canada by Best Book Manufacturers inc.

Contents

PREFACE

Reading with the Troubled Reader is intended for all educators, although it is particularly directed to reading resource personnel, classroom and student teachers, and parents.

I have several purposes for writing the book. First, I regularly make presentations on the topic at conferences, and after almost every lecture I'm asked if there is a book that links troubled readers with a holistic approach to literacy. To my knowledge there is not, although various writers touch on parts of the subject.

Some deny that there is any such thing as a troubled reader. I think the day will come when that's very close to being true, but it certainly isn't now. Which brings me to my second purpose: to describe a transition between what is and what I believe can be. It's an attempt to change the way we view reading difficulties both in the resource room and in the classroom, and because I view it as part of a transition, I look forward to its obsolescence: I *want* it to be outgrown.

My approach has its base in the "whole language" philosophy of facilitating literacy acquisition, a philosophy that makes one important assumption: that all children can become literate, easily and enthusiastically, in the same kind of environment and with the same kind of support systems that enable them to learn to walk, talk, climb and ride a bike. I believe that when classroom and resource room practices fully accommodate what we now know about learning written language, only about one percent of the school population will be "troubled readers," children who truly have a learning style that makes the linear-sequential nature of reading difficult for them to master. And I believe that

1

even these children, given alternatives to print during the extra time they need to become fully literate, will be able to learn everything everyone else learns in school. The others will learn to read as easily as they learned to speak.

Thirdly, this book seeks to bring together whole language teachers and those researchers who are studying the physiological causes of learning difficulties. The whole language camp tends to deny that there can be physiological causes for difficulty in learning to read, while the scientists claim that handicapped learners are being deprived of the skills they need. I've put my foot in both camps, and it seems to me that each needs to learn from the other. They both need to broaden their definitions and understandings of learners and of the reading process. We have no right to prolong the suffering of children by being stubborn and narrow-minded.

My final purpose is personal and flows out of a statement Gordon Wells made in an address given at the 1987 annual conference of the International Reading Association. He said:

> Writing in particular enables us to record our thoughts so that we can recapture them and look at them critically, so that we can, if you like, bootstrap our own thinking by means of putting it down for inspection.

This book is a personal consolidation of my understandings at the moment and an expression of my major professional interest. It is a manifestation of my need to communicate and to share. Some of my conclusions are tentative, some of my "causes" speculative. I don't have all the answers—and my research has shown me that no one else does either. I added to my knowledge and modified my perspectives even as I wrote, and I intend to continue my own process of growth and change. This book is a footprint in my journey.

CHAPTER 1

OVERVIEW

My main purpose in *Reading with the Troubled Reader* is to describe ways of recognizing and helping different types of troubled readers. First, however, I want to explore what reading is and how it happens, in particular for those children who come to school already reading. Because these early readers have learned naturally, we can discover from watching them how reading is most easily learned.

Following that is a list and description of what I call "universal reading principles," principles I believe apply to *all* readers, troubled or not. They form the pillars of the reading process and are the most important elements to emphasize in any discussion about teaching reading. I hope that chapter will become the most dog-eared section in your copy of the book!

The next chapters describe five types of troubled readers. Three of those descriptions are elaborations and extensions of categories included in Don Holdaway's discussion of diagnostic teaching (1979). The remaining two categories I've added from my own experience.

Sharing what I've learned about those children I call "global learners" is especially important to me since they are the ones I feel are most at risk in both traditional and whole language classrooms—and the ones, perhaps, who will benefit most from a better and broader understanding of learning patterns. Much research is being done in that area, and I've tried to provide enough detail to challenge you to look more closely at your existing beliefs and practices. That chapter is therefore quite long; nevertheless, the heart of my statement lies there and I urge you not to ignore it.

For each category I include:

- one or more reading samples from troubled readers in that category (I've changed the names of the children to ensure their anonymity);
- a description of the characteristics and behavior typical of that type of troubled reader;
- possible causes of the trouble;
- suggestions for helping;
- additional comments (sometimes).

At the end I provide a descriptive glossary of terms for those readers who aren't familiar with the jargon of the whole language approach. I'm not fond of jargon—I guess no one is— but it *can* make communication more efficient. Because invented terms have a tendency to change and evolve, however, I emphasize that the definitions are strictly my own understandings of the meanings of those terms as I use them in *this* book. You may find they have different meanings in other contexts.

Suggestions for further reading, including in-depth coverage of the theoretical framework behind whole language teaching, are found in the bibliography. Finally, an index has been added to help readers quickly reference important terms and concepts.

CAUTION: LABEL LIBEL

Please understand that I consider categorizing, typecasting or otherwise labeling children a potentially harmful thing to do. Categories are useful for identifying needs only in the most general way. Labels should simply identify *processes of learning,* not peg children as intrinsically inadequate. "Learning disabled," for example, is such a damning label. Children who have the kinds of learning differences LD testing usually uncovers can indeed be at a disadvantage when it comes to some of the standard academic performance requirements of school. There is no denying that their processing style is different from the "norm." But when the label forces them to be subjected to instructional programs that methodically prevent them from using their strengths, it's as crippling as their troubles. I prefer a label that tells us how they *do* learn, what they *can* do. I call them "global learners," a term that acknowledges that they *are* learners and hints at how I think they approach learning.

"Dyslexic" is another label that tells me nothing about the nature of the child's reading problem. In Webster's Unabridged, dyslexia is defined as "a disturbance of the ability to read." All that label tells me, the teacher who must help, is that the child is having trouble reading; it doesn't tell me what I need to do to help. I once heard David Doake define dyslexia as "a name in search of a disease"! On the other hand, a term like Don Holdaway's "underpredictive" tells just which part of the reading process is not working efficiently. If I can trust the assessment, I can start a recovery procedure immediately.

INDIVIDUALIZATION: THE KEY

Before I work with any child individually I want to have a general idea of what *that* child is doing. If you use this book as a reference, please tailor every suggestion I offer to the specific needs of the child you are working with. Some children need to be pushed; some need only the slightest nudge; some push themselves too hard and need to be encouraged to relax. Finding the balance that will build confidence and support success is the central goal of my own recovery work. I force myself to ignore all grade-level "standards" and other standardized measures of achievement. I measure each child's progress solely against that child's own baseline and in terms of that child's learning pace.

I work using two principles. First, once I've decided where the child's processing is weak, I stop generalizing and focus on the individual. I try to mold my responses and nudgings to the child's personality. I try to create an environment that results in success. Second, I don't single out one particular helping strategy or technique and beat it to death. I try to work on every strategy and skill the child is ready for in a given session. If you take a close look at my responses in some of the samples, you will see that I use several techniques on a moment-by-moment basis as the child is reading.

CHAPTER 2

EARLY READERS

Kindergarten and grade one teachers always seem to have one or more children who enter their classes already reading. Thirty years ago such children were an irritant, evidence that the teacher wasn't always a necessary ingredient. Often the parents didn't understand how such a miracle could have happened and worried about the treatment their children would receive when the teacher discovered they were early readers. They didn't praise their children or let them know the significance of their accomplishment; they simply kept their joy to themselves and hoped for the best. Today's teachers have better training in educational psychology, and more and more teachers who understand how reading is learned are being placed at the kindergarten and grade one levels.

But how do these children do it? How can a process as complex as learning to read be mastered without instruction? And why don't all children learn to read early? These questions have probably been asked for as long as literacy has been considered a desirable asset, but it has only been in this century that early readers have been examined for what they can tell us about *teaching* reading.

"READINESS" BEGINS AT BIRTH

Reading is a highly complex language process, not simply a strict left-to-right decoding of letters to sounds. It involves several mental activities that take place almost simultaneously, bringing into use the many "sub-stations" in the brain that are responsible for various aspects of reception, transmission, processing, association and expression.

Almost everyone comes to the task of learning to read already having mastered an even harder task: learning to speak. Unless born profoundly deaf or otherwise severely handicapped, every child learns to manipulate a complex of noises in an almost infinite arrangement of patterns, each set of which, in its appropriate context, conveys meaning to other people. It's a symbol system: orally conveyed and aurally received words and combinations of words stand for things, people, actions and—most remarkable of all—ideas. Even children under two can label and understand complex abstracts like "goodbye" and "happy" and "danger."

For oral language we employ background knowledge, awareness of grammatical patterns, and intentions or predictions of meaning. These are the backbone of language—not just speaking, but all language activities including reading, writing and non-verbal or non-literate communication such as body language, dance, music, art and mime. Most children are proficient language users by the time they reach school age. When they are allowed to bring all this experience to learning to read, gaining control over the process is relatively easy and quick for most.

THE READING PROCESS

Goodman and Burke (1980) identified three separate operations within the reading process—prediction, confirmation and integration—which I view as working in constantly interacting loops of propulsion, trouble-shooting and growth.

Prediction

Prediction involves setting expectations for the meaning a particular text will provide. I think of it as the fuel that keeps us moving through a text—the anticipation of what's to come that drives us forward. As proficient readers, the expectations we have will depend on a number of factors:

The nature of the material

I will make very different predictions about the type of information I expect to get from a magazine article and a telephone directory.

The circumstances surrounding our reading

I will give very different attention to a magazine article recommended by a friend than to one skimmed through in the dentist's office.

Our purpose for reading

In reading a friend's article I will be keeping in mind my friend's tastes and reasons for recommending it, and be anticipating a discussion of the content afterwards. If I'm reading the article as support for a research paper, the information I choose for a focus may be quite different.

The format or visual arrangement of the text

Previous experiences with a wide variety of formats helps us make at-a-glance predictions about the content of a text. Compare a calendar and a recipe card, for example: you expect the kind, number and arrangement of words and numerals in these two types of text to be very different.

Our knowledge of language

Reading requires using our awareness of the grammatical patterns and logic of our language, together with our bank of automatically recognized sight words. Our experience with spoken language would preclude the prediction that the word *the,* for example, which we know by sight, would be followed by the word *went.* It doesn't sound like real language; it's not grammatical.

Confirmation

Confirmation is the process of checking predictions against the text. As long as the flow of meaning is maintained, we don't stop to focus closely on details of print: we sample the text in chunks. Miscues are made but uncorrected. When meaning is lost, or a sentence or phrase doesn't register as real language, we go back and look more closely at the text to see where the problem occurred. If necessary, we telescope in and examine initial letter sounds and blends, word configuration, outstanding features, prefixes, affixes and syllabic "chunks." If we have too many difficulties with a text, we abandon it altogether.

Integration

Integration is the process of choosing and incorporating information from the text into our store of knowledge and ideas. Goodman and Burke emphasize that our choices are based on our purposes for reading and our belief system, or world view. Growth occurs when our reading results in a change in our belief system.

CONDITIONS FOR EARLY READING

It is no more reasonable to expect all, or even very many, children to read before school-age than it is to expect all children to walk by eight months. There are general time periods when the largest numbers of children are most receptive to learning certain kinds of activities or processes, although the range among individuals is very wide. The fact that it's possible for a fairly regular percentage of children to read early doesn't mean that all are ready, even given perfect environmental conditions. But early readers do teach us how reading is most easily learned and what conditions contribute to facilitating the process.

For children to gain control over the reading process without formal instruction or planned guidance, the following combination of factors is important: a strong interest in language and books; a positive, supportive, book-oriented environment; and maturity in the ability to process visual symbols.

Natural Interest in Literacy

Just as some children are fascinated by machines, dolls or climbing trees, so others are intensely curious about language, books and print. One of the ingredients of early reading is an intense curiosity about and desire to master written language. Early readers, and those who catch the bug particularly seriously in kindergarten or grade one, can become absolute *pests* in their drive to read! They concentrate intensely, they nag for information and they ignore suggestions, even directives, to do other things. It's almost a compulsion! And their interest is reinforced when the people in their environment answer them directly and immediately, no strings attached, no follow-up interference.

I can remember my own early associations with books. Margaret Wise Brown's *The Golden Egg Book* has such strong emotional associations that it brought tears to my eyes when I saw it back in print a few years ago. My mother read it to me over and over again and I studied the wonderful pictures and intricate borders and thought about the gentle, comforting story for hours when I was alone with the book. Then came the day—I remember the day, during one of my "study" periods—when my attention went to the words

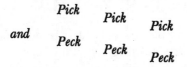

written down across the page. I already *knew* what the words were for that page—I had heard them so many times—but on that day I *noticed* them. It was not an overwhelming thrill, a "Eureka, I can read!" sort of thing. In fact I didn't realize that's what was happening at all. It was simply another detail I had discovered, like the details in the pictures. I remember taking the book to my mother and asking her to confirm that those words were *Pick Pick Pick*—which, of course, she did. From then on, print held as much fascination as pictures. It was as simple as that. I have no idea when I could have been considered a reader. I didn't consider *myself* one until I had been through several volumes of *Dick and Jane*.

Supportive Environment

Exposure to books

The first characteristic of an early reading environment is the availability of books and the regular modeling of reading. A home library and frequent trips to the public library provide the materials; being read to and seeing others read provide the necessary modeling. "Others," of course, include more than just parents. When grandparents, babysitters and older siblings provide the modeling, children can become readers without their parents even noticing.

Doake (1988) points out the importance of reading aloud to young children. It not only orients them to books and their conventions (front/back, left/right, top/bottom, pictures/text), but it gradually helps them become aware that *text* carries the message and that written language has different patterns and structures from oral language.

Part of the process involves the repetition of favorite stories. Early readers ask to hear their favorites dozens of times, so they know even a long story well enough to correct any reader who miscues. (My son memorized Dr. Seuss's *Green Eggs and Ham* in this way. Sometimes I would get so sick of the story I'd try to skip pages, but I never got away with it!) Emergent readers gradually start matching the print to their memory-based reconstruction of the text, absorbing sight words, punctuation conventions and letter-sound correspondences as they go. It's this gradual process of being drawn into involvement with print that creates early readers.

Time for practice

Early readers have been characteristically left alone to look at books and practice the reading-like behaviors that have been modeled for them. The books in their houses are accessible and inviting at all times, not kept on a high shelf to be chosen by someone else at selected times. They can take a "book break" whenever they wish and choose their favorites over and over. They have the peace and leisure, the uninterrupted chunks of time, to be involved in their interests. I saw a photo of my niece at age two sitting in an armchair totally absorbed in *Each Peach Pear Plum*. She is clearly unaware of the photographer or anything else around her. The book is upside down.

Freedom from interference

Children who become early readers are *allowed* to learn, are *free* to learn. No one hovers over them, monitors their efforts to read, is anxious about every skipped, mispronounced or substituted word. No one pressures them to "sound it out." Since our culture doesn't expect preschoolers to read, parents don't feel a need to push them in the area of literacy. They are pleased when children show an interest in books, they answer their questions and make casual observations about print, but they don't deliberately *teach* reading. The children are simply supported and left alone. The parents are handy resources, providers of good books and regular models of good reading. They are discussion-mates, hint-givers and listeners. They read alphabet books and show their children how to write their names and other words that arouse their curiosity. They give them lots of paper and writing implements and don't criticize their efforts or deny their claims to be authors and artists. Often the parents are grateful for the time *they* have for themselves while their children are concentrating quietly in another room for long periods. They are too busy themselves to notice the little increments of progress that are being made behind their backs until suddenly one day Junior rattles off the printing on the back of a cereal box.

Emotional stability

In addition to being motivated and physiologically ready (see below) for learning, the learner must be in an environment that offers opportunities to explore and learn, that encourages risk-taking while providing supportive safety nets. Children who spend their infancy in playpens will not receive the broad sensory stimulus that a free-roaming child gets. Children growing up in violence or confusion will be spending their energy trying to sort out the emotional environment instead of developing relationships with the physical world. All other conditions being equal, if children are suffering from emotional imbalance, whatever the cause, they haven't the ability to concentrate, to commit themselves to a major new learning enterprise. In fact new ideas, new risks, are a threat to their already shaky sense of security. It's my experience that for any learning task to be accomplished comfortably, emotional problems must be cleared up first. Emotionally, too, children need to be *free* to learn.

Positive emotional associations

Being read to by an adult or sibling with whom there is already a loving bond creates an association between books and pleasure. Stories are heard in a secure, snuggly, sharing atmosphere, an atmosphere children want to recreate for themselves when the adults aren't available. Just as negative associations from early traumatic experiences can result in life-long avoidance behaviors, even recurring visits to the psychiatrist, so positive associations can keep us seeking the conditions that surrounded those early experiences. The association can be so strong that some people, myself included, find it hard to go to sleep at night if they haven't read to themselves for a few minutes before turning out the light. Reading becomes a sort of life-long security blanket!

Early Maturing Integrational System

Itskoff (1986) gives us one view of learning – any learning. He suggests that learning contains three systems: the sensory, the semantic and the integrational.

The *sensory* system provides the raw information. Auditory input is especially important for learning language and is the precursor to learning to read. Reading is the visual representation of a process already mastered through sound. It is easier for the blind to learn to read than the deaf, because blind people have learned the structures and auditory representations of language naturally, using the sense that was refined for that purpose. The profoundly deaf haven't had those five years or so of intensive prior experience in learning our highly complex communication system. They are faced with the double task of mastering, late and laboriously, the structures, sequences and meanings of language while at the same time learning the visual symbol system that represents those meanings.

The *semantic* system is the system that allows learners to discover some form of meaning for themselves out of the sensory input. Humans are driven to understand their world. The brain categorizes experiences, makes associations and connections, and creates new awarenesses out of the combinations within itself. Everything we do is motivated by our drive to discover, create or maintain meaning, or to discard, avoid or reject nonsense or confusion.

The *integrational* system organizes and presents the sensory information in such a way that the semantic system can make sense of it. Through a variety of nerve networks, connecting many "sub-contractors" in the process, sensory information is sorted and sent out to the appropriate centers for inclusion in our store of knowledge and our world view.

All physically and emotionally normal children are aware of sensory stimuli and naturally possessed of a drive to understand their world. The drive for meaning results in a gradual expansion of the ability to make sense of the sensory input, which in turn results in the development and refinement of the integrational system. But the integrational system takes time to perfect, so children interpret and refine at different ages and in different areas. To learn to switch over from a sound-based symbol system (spoken language) to a visually-based one (written language) requires more refined use of the visual aspect of the integrational system, and most children don't seem to develop that refinement until they are between six and eight years old. Since this "readiness" coincides with a developmental brain-growth spurt, that may mean most children *can't* learn to read until this age: their brains simply don't have the proper neural connections before that. Clearly this isn't the case with early readers. Their integrational systems apparently mature earlier than average.

ADVENT OF CHANGE

For a long time, reading instruction in North America was based on an analysis of language—its structures, patterns and rules. It assumed that "small is easy": the smaller the visual or phonic unit a child has to cope with, the easier it is to learn. It also assumed that reading is best learned through a cumulative, logically sequenced exposure to rules and patterns.

Recent research is teaching us that the opposite is true. Early readers and writers first "adopt" or take ownership of a whole piece of literature — a favorite poem or story — and then, through repeated exposure and personally directed practice, gradually refine their mastery. They pick up sight words and absorb rules and patterns as they interact with texts. There is no set logical or developmental sequence governing which patterns or rules they discover first, nor do they necessarily learn short sight words before long ones. In fact, their learning is more governed by impact than by logic. They remember the meaningful, the outstanding and the useful first, and those are all determined by personal interest and purpose.

Educators have started applying in the classroom the knowledge we have gained from this sort of research. Individual teachers, schools and even whole districts, provinces and states are making it their policy to approach literacy acquisition from whole to part. It is not my purpose in this book to detail at length the "how to" of such approaches: included in the bibliography are books that explain procedures. However, I do attempt to base my suggestions for working with troubled readers on the knowledge and insights this research has given me.

CHAPTER 3

UNIVERSAL READING PRINCIPLES

Watching early readers makes clear that certain principles are foundational to the learning of reading. If what happens in the homes as these children move toward literacy is replicated in the classroom for slower maturing readers, those principles will ensure that comfortable learning occurs there as well. When past experiences or physiologically based differences have created troubled readers, however, a concentrated focus on specific support techniques is necessary for the recovery process.

My descriptions here of the "universal" principles are deliberately slanted toward their application to troubled readers, although the implications for all readers are apparent.

CONFIDENCE

Confidence is one of the most significant factors in a child's development as a reader. Troubled readers almost always see themselves as poor readers. They show fear and anxiety, or reject reading altogether as not worth the effort. Therefore, I make sure that I don't put these children in situations that might confirm their own suspicions.

I don't ask children to read orally in public until they have had ample opportunity to practice a passage privately first, after exposure through supported reading techniques. When I do ask them to read aloud, I don't butt in immediately when they make a mistake, even when it causes meaning loss. By waiting until further reading has provided enough context to trigger their recognition of the meaning loss, I give them an opportunity to self-correct.

Even then I try to be gentle by saying something like, "Back there you read that the goats ate grease. I thought that was a rather odd idea. What do you think?" If they don't go back and reread or make the correction orally on the spot, if they just shrug and say, "I don't know," then I say, "Let's go back to that part and take another look." I try not to say things like, "You missed that word. What did you do wrong?" When meaning is maintained I don't interfere at all, unless I want them to notice how they've used their knowledge of language in processing the print. They need regular successes. In the early stages of recovery work it's preferable to help them master more short books than fewer long ones.

ENJOYMENT

Competent readers are avid readers. For them, reading is a pleasure. They freely choose what they want to read to satisfy their curiosity or entertain themselves.

It's my experience that children who don't enjoy reading limit their reading to what school or home requires. Previous experiences of frustration, failure and humiliation outweigh any pleasure they may have received. So when I begin recovery work with these children, I see that the majority of their reading experiences are enjoyable. I make sure they feel some purpose in the activity: to entertain themselves or others, to accomplish an activity (cooking, playing a game, following directions to make something, etc.) or to obtain information. At the same time, I see that most of the text they encounter is easy, especially in the beginning, by:

- finding non-contrived high-interest material as close to their independent level as possible;
- ensuring that their reading time is full of pleasure and free of interference;

- keeping strategy lessons short and relevant to the immediate problem;
- making entertainment or information-gathering the purpose, not the act of reading itself.

OWNERSHIP

Personal response and interaction are important for all readers.

Integrating Background Knowledge

I promote discussion with my beginning readers before, during and after reading books. I particularly encourage them to speculate on what they think will happen, or why something did happen, based on their own experiences and feelings, triggered by the text.

At the beginning of a reading the children use their background knowledge to predict. During the reading they predict and confirm, learn new perspectives or information, and become hooked on the book by becoming involved with the content. At the end they confirm their first predictions and, if they have become sufficiently "caught," decide to experience the book again, or a similar one.

Encouraging readers to connect their own experiences with the text helps them understand that reading is a process of expanding their lives. It's important that they come to see reading as a source of personal growth, of needed answers or interesting questions — and that they aren't alone with their fears and joys, their problems and quests. If they learn that early, reading will become a lifelong habit.

Retelling

Most readers enjoy telling someone else about the stories they read. Asking troubled readers to recall a story focuses them on meaning; encouraging them to relate it to their own experience involves them personally in the content. In the process they learn that I value overall meaning, and I learn what sorts of things are important to them. I use their retellings not only to assess what they get out of their reading, but to help me in selecting additional material that will interest them. I avoid leading questions, which simply set up expectations of what *I* (or the publisher, if the questions are from a directed reading lesson) think is important to remember.

SIGHT-WORD RECOGNITION

Fluent reading requires a reasonable bank of automatic sight words, and most troubled readers have too small a bank. Many common support words in English (*what, come, said, there,* etc.) don't conform easily to language rules or patterns and need to be memorized by sight. In recovery work I avoid using lists of words in isolation; practice in using basic sight words is most effective when done from context. I use a variety of ways for achieving this end.

Choice of Materials

I choose materials that use the basic sight words in abundance, but in a natural or predictable way. Selected books from *Story Box* and *Bookshelf* and trade books from the bookstore or library (for instance some of the Dr. Seuss books) work well when children are allowed to choose from among them. The more children read, the more they absorb and remember the most common words. I encourage them to read the books again and again until there is nothing more they want from them. Some children will cling to a few titles for a long time; they are building confidence and security.

It's also important to keep introducing new books so the children experience the basic words in a variety of literature settings and have a source of choices to avoid boredom. However, if the book they choose for pleasure is the same "old favorite" for some time, I spend at least a portion of the session with that book. I try to set up other natural situations that allow for repeated readings as well, such as reading to younger children who come to visit.

Cloze Practice

I make up cloze (fill in the blanks) sentences and short stories, or use the pattern of a favorite predictable story, leaving out the words that are currently under focus. These I list at the top of the page, along the right margin or, in the case of a booklet, on a separate sheet of paper. I make sure that the sentences are unambiguous and the text highly supportive of the word that would meaningfully fill the blank.

Focus on Word Families

Because I don't want to break the train of thought in the reading process too often, I use this technique only occasionally and not at all with very early readers. For words that are members of a large word family, such as *pat,* I point out the association with a known word from that family *(cat)* and then brainstorm a list of other rhyming words from the same family, placing the known ones at the top. When the children have trouble with a word from the family, I have them quickly read part of the list to identify the unknown and help make the association between the known and the unknown. Sometimes it's sufficient to say, "That word rhymes with _____."

Words in Isolation

When I do use words in isolation, I adapt a system designed by Holdaway (1980). I put on separate file cards five or six words that are repeated throughout a familiar text, noting in the corner the pages where those words occur. After the children finish reading their stories, we go through the packs and make two piles, one of words they know and one of words they're working on. They match the latter to the text and reread up to the word to provide the context. I encourage them to provide a context on the back of the card as well, to help them identify the word the next time they need to. One way is to draw a picture or a symbol that represents the title of the book. For some that's enough to recall the word; for others it's a reminder of which book to reach for to read back the sentence containing the word. Another way is to write or dictate a short, simple sentence containing the word, underlined. When the children next practice their words, if they can't remember the word in isolation they can read their sentence for help.

In general I consider words "learned" when the children have identified them in isolation during three separate but consecutive sessions. However, this rule of thumb varies for individuals, particularly for global learners. I periodically initiate reviews and return forgotten words to the pack for another round.

Holdaway lists 406 basic sight words, accompanied by simple sentences. Those words can be put on cards, with the sentences on the back, and used for practice with older troubled readers. One school system I know has even computerized the system!

STRATEGIES

Strategies are plans of action readers use for dealing with unknown words and with confusion when meaning isn't clear. They are the grease that keeps the reading process running smoothly. Strategies are more important than specific word-attack skills because they keep the meaning of the whole in mind and that, after all, is the driving force behind the reading act in the first place.

Blanking

Blanking is simply reading ahead. A form of oral cloze, it introduces more context clues for the unknown word. I model this strategy for the whole class by preparing enlarged print material with blank spaces in the text. When we read it together we say "blank," adding whatever ending is grammatically appropriate. Then we go back and find a meaningful word for the blank. For example:

> I was (blanking) down the road.
> Then I saw a little toad.
> I caught it.
> I picked it up.
> I put it in a cage.

When the children read with me one-on-one, I remind them of the strategy: say "blank" for any unknown word, read on and then go back to try out possibilities that might fit, with or without consideration for graphic cues.

Cloze

Cloze is one of the most important techniques for reinforcing the idea that individual words and groups of words contribute to a meaningful whole. While reinforcing both prediction and confirmation, cloze provides the psychological satisfaction of having completed something.

There are many cloze variations. Blanking is one. Traditional fill-in-the-blanks exercises in the workbooks of basal programs are cloze exercises. Leaving out phrases as well as words, leaving sentences unfinished, giving graphophonic cues such as initial letters, blends, syllables or endings (-ing, -ed or -s) are variations. Putting in an obscure, foreign or nonsense word and asking the children to define it based on context is a cloze technique. (I don't use nonsense words myself, since I don't want to imply that reading is nonsense.)

To aid prediction I provide a highly supportive context *before* the missing word or phrase. For confirmation I have true indicators of what would make sense *follow* the space. If I want to call attention in particular to the graphophonic cueing system I provide the letter or morpheme in the appropriate part of the space. If I want to reinforce sight words or word families I provide a text with those words listed in the margin, to be written into the blanks.

Cloze exercises are usually fun because meaning is created in the doing, especially if the children's own words are permitted. *Mad Libs,* freely found in airport and bus terminal magazine stores, are cloze booklets that require the use of a certain part of speech to fill each blank. I once used one when I had to fill in unexpectedly in a grade six class. The children were literally rolling in the aisles, some laughing so hard they had tears streaming down their faces as I read them the passages after they had given me their word choices.

Rerunning

Rerunning means rereading a string of words, perhaps even the whole first part of the page, in order to re-establish the semantic and grammatical flow. I ask children to rerun when they have lost their place, encountered an unknown word or become confused.

I prefer to *model* this strategy rather than instruct it directly. For example, during the daily choral reading of an enlarged-print text we often stop to examine illustrations, discuss an interesting aspect of print, talk about the story events, or relate our own background knowledge and feelings to the story. When we get back to reading the text I always rerun the last line or two to re-establish the flow. I also model the practice when I find myself making a mistake or losing meaning while reading.

In the early stages of recovery work I often rerun some of the previously read text when the children are stopped by a word for too long, to help them establish the semantic and grammatical structures that will provide the context for more efficient prediction. Later, when reading and confidence are stronger, I suggest, "Why don't you go back to there and read that part again to get the flow back?"

Substitutions

Efficient readers, when they are engrossed in the text and reading quickly, often make substitutions without realizing they have done so. Making substitutions can be an acceptable conscious strategy as well. How many of us have made up a name to substitute for a foreign one we've encountered in a novel? But some children, particularly those who are overly conscientious or visually acute, or those who have been taught that reading is an exacting process of individual word identification, hesitate to use this strategy. We need to let them know what to do when they want to continue reading and there's no dictionary or handy mature reader to tell them the unknown word. They need to know that it's not necessary to come to a standstill over unfamiliar or unfathomable words, that substituting other words that make sense is acceptable.

In addition to cloze techniques, I encourage substituting in a number of ways:
• We do group rewrites of favorite texts. Using the same pattern as the original, we replace content words with our own choices.
• We personalize songs and poems. For example, I tape clear

plastic over the words *Brother John* on my enlarged-print chart of the English version of *Frère Jacques* and we take turns substituting the names of the boys in the class.

- I put a cloze version of a new poem on an overhead transparency and tell the children we'll fill in the blanks and then compare our version with the original to see which we like better (usually ours!).
- I use white Post-it tape to cover words in a big book, which the class then alters and sends to another class for reading.

During one-to-one sessions I always encourage substitutions if I know the child doesn't yet have other skills or strategies for identifying the word.

SUPPORTED READING

Supported reading is what happens naturally when developing readers, sharing books with supportive adults, begin to take control of the reading process. It is a form of low-risk reading that provides another voice (or voices) to carry the weight of the reading while the children chime in wherever they know the material. As the readers mature, it allows them to experience fluency, intonation, eye movement, etc. — that is, *enjoyable* reading — without the psychological burden of having to perform (and be judged) alone. Miscues are lost or diminished by the other voice(s) and by the attention the lead reader, usually the teacher, maintains on the content of the story. One-to-one assisted reading, choral reading, echo reading, peer reading and taped stories are all forms of supported reading.

Assisted Reading

The *general* procedure goes like this: I ask a child to choose a favorite book, brought from home or picked from a collection of predictable books in my room. I read it though first. We focus on the story, the pictures, the ideas, our opinions, reactions, speculations and judgments, as well as on details we think are interesting or relevant. (I don't think it's necessary or desirable to limit higher order thinking to more mature readers. Ability to think has nothing to do with reading maturity!) We *enjoy* the story.

As I read it the second time I do more voice-matching and use oral cloze frequently in places where the fill-in is highly predictable, as in the last words of a repeated refrain or where a rhyming word would be obvious. I occasionally ask the child to point to a word in the text that I'm sure is easy to find.

The next time I ask the child to read with me and do the pointing. I am very conscious of his or her needs in relation to that particular text. I keep my voice a bit louder if the child finds the book difficult; I read just under the reader's voice if he or she is more comfortable, using my voice as a safety net; and I whisper when the material is easy, or simply offer an occasional hint about a word by means of the carefully timed voicing of an initial sound.

Timing is very important: I can diminish initiative and problem-solving efforts by coming in too soon or cause frustration by waiting so long that meaning flow and a sense of success are lost. And timing has to be adjusted not only for the different kinds of texts used, but for each personality I work with.

Choral Reading

I use this term to refer to group participation in the reading of a text that is presented in enlarged print, either as a commercial or class-made "big book," or on chart paper or the chalkboard, or projected with an opaque or overhead projector. During the initial readings my voice, and the voices of the children who can already read the text, dominate. The others listen and chime in as they feel confident and comfortable. During subsequent readings I gradually turn more of the text over to the children, using oral cloze, encouraging them to take parts, etc. My role becomes one of regulating the reading pace by continuing to point as they read.

Choral reading promotes a sense of community — group enthusiasm is contagious — and invites discussion of both the content and the print details, allowing the children to learn what they are curious about and ready for. The children become familiar with and participate in the reading of large numbers of texts they wouldn't be able to read on their own. They are willing to take risks when the "group voice" drowns out potentially embarrassing misreadings.

Echo Reading

In echo reading the lead reader reads aloud a section of text and the child's voice follows right after. It's a way of familiarizing children with a text close enough to their instructional level that they need only one or two encounters with it before tackling it on their own. I use this mainly with older troubled readers who have gained a good measure of confidence and are concentrating on refining skills and strategies using only slightly familiar texts. I vary the length of text to be read according to the difficulty of the text, the short-term memory capacity and the confidence level of a particular child.

Peer Reading

During reading practice times my children often get together in pairs or small groups to choral-read books on their own. Because they have had extensive modeling from me and their kindergarten teachers, they accept each other's miscues and thus create low-risk supported reading situations for themselves. They don't always stick to choral reading, especially when there are substantial gaps in reading maturity. Sometimes more mature readers will take on the role of the lead reader or will simply help the less mature readers along. Sometimes more and less mature readers read alternate pages; sometimes they take turns reading to each other from different books; and sometimes they move in and out of choral and individual reading. The delight is that friendship seems to prevent embarrassment or humiliation, even when two or three readers are adamantly correcting each other or arguing about a word. Children seem to have a sense of the equality of their own authority among peers which allows them to freely learn and share with each other.

Taped Stories

Some children learn to read stories by listening to them on tape while following the text in the book, a form of one-to-one echo reading. Carbo (1985) advocates using individually paced recordings of text as the principle remediation technique. However, even with responsibility for anywhere from 20 to 35 children I find it takes as much time to prepare the tapes as it does to work person-to-person, where I can do on-the-spot coaching as I go along. Some children, especially overpredictive readers, don't attend to print as they listen. They become familiar with the story but not the matching print. Still, taped listening sessions are valuable for familiarizing readers with a story, reinforcing independent practice, helping them learn to attend and simply exposing them to more literature. I have always had a listening center in my classroom and have encouraged its use.

WRITING

The beauty of encouraging children to write is that they learn so much about print in the process. Reading and writing go hand in hand. They feed each other. Writers are readers of their own texts; readers read the writings of their peers. Writing contributes to left-to-right sequencing in a very concrete way. Invented spelling encourages children to think about the way words look and sound. The more they have to use written language for their own purposes and expression, the more they attend to print to improve their efficiency and accuracy.

Ironically, troubled readers who have not had to do much writing seem more amenable to the idea than those on whom it has been imposed in the past. If perfection in spelling and handwriting is demanded, writing becomes an impossible task of trying to remember too many things at once: the letters for a word, their proper sequence, when and where to use upper and lower case, spacing, punctuation, how to size and form the letters on the lines and, finally, just what it was they wanted to say! But if mechanical details are postponed and the initial focus is simply on getting ideas down on paper to remember them for later sharing, writing can become a joyful activity. Troubled literacy learners need all the joy they can get.

Children need to feel that writing is a purposeful activity. Here are some examples of functional purposes in the lives of children:
- shopping lists, particularly for things they want to buy or be given (clothes, toys, etc.);

- memos and reminders to others for events, appointments, etc. they want to attend;
- signs (*Wet Paint, Keep Out,* etc.);
- invitations to friends by mail;
- a diary (of a trip, etc.) to share later with a grandparent or other close person;
- instructions for playing a game, operating a machine or toy, constructing something or cooking a favorite treat;
- an account of a personal experience, an expository text on a subject they know well, or a fiction story, to be published and shared with the rest of the class;
- communication with a distant friend, relative or penpal with the hope of receiving a reply;
- a record of the scores of sports events.

I have found incentives helpful for children who are particularly resistant to being overloaded. I offer to type final drafts of their letters to friends or relatives in standard spelling to remove the burden of recopying. (One year I had a child for whom writing to his grandmother was so important that I walked him to the post office each week and bought a stamp for him so he could personally mail his letters. There was something viscerally important to him about licking the stamp and dropping that letter into the slot.)

I (or parent volunteers) take care of "publishing" stories, poems or accounts to add to the class library. Alternating between taking dictation and having them write a few words is a way to start some children. I also find that making cloze booklets based on familiar story patterns reduces the burden of too much writing. The children can create their own versions of a story by writing only a few words per page, and in the process they have provided themselves with some reading material!

A word processing software program for an available computer motivates even the most reluctant writers. One year I was also made the overseer of the computer room, next to mine. It turned out to be a golden year for my children, who were able to print out their work almost every time they came to me. In addition to the motivation it provided, the computer seemed a special help to those older children for whom poor spelling was an issue. I am convinced that that was partly because handwriting is so visually different from printed text. Those children found it impossible to recognize misspelled words when they wrote them out by hand, but could see the errors when the words were typed in the standard print form they were accustomed to seeing (and remembering) in textbooks, spelling lists and reading materials. Also, typing is easier in terms of fine motor coordination than writing by hand, and making corrections is fun rather than a burden.

If you have access to *Print Shop* or *Newsroom* programs when you are working with a group of troubled readers, writing and editing a newspaper is a great incentive.

CHAPTER 4

STRATEGY DEPENDENT READERS

EXAMPLE: RICKY

Ricky is in the last quarter of grade one, in a whole language classroom. He loves the shared language period and gets very involved in the stories, chants and songs. But his teacher referred him to me because, although she felt he was ready to move out of the emergent stage, he seemed to be having trouble doing so. I asked him to choose one of three stories I knew he had read with the class several times during the group language sessions. He chose *I Was Walking Down the Road* by Sarah Barchas and started out reading steadily and smoothly, running his finger under the lines of print.

Text	Ricky
I was walking down the road.	I was walking down the road.
Then I saw a little toad.	Then I saw a little toad.
I caught it.	I caught it.
I picked it up.	I picked it up.
I put it in a cage.	I put it in a cage.

I was looking at the sky.	I was looking up at the sky.
Then I saw a butterfly.	When I saw a little butterfly.
I caught it.	I caught it.
I picked it up.	I picked it up.
I put it in a cage.	I put it in a cage.
I was working with a rake.	I was raking . . . [now pointing
Then I saw a little snake.	carefully to each word] I was
I caught it.	raking with a rake . . . No! [again,
I picked it up.	more slowly, pointing] I . . . was
I put it in a cage.	. . . raking . . . [pointing to *work-*
	ing] What's that word?

T: What does it start with?
R: W.
T: What's the sound of *w*?
R: Um . . . I don't know . . . /l/ [sounded]?
T: It's /w/ [sounded]. Does that help you?
R: I was . . . No [clearly frustrated]. I can't remember what goes there.
T: I'll help. I was /w/ . . . [stretching the sound a bit].
R: Oh! Working! I was *working* with a rake when I saw a little snake .

DISCUSSION

Ricky knows what reading is all about, that print carries the message. So he proceeded from top to bottom, left to right, and was able to word-voice match accurately, even with multisyllabic words, although the second verse shows that he wasn't bound by it. But in the third verse he got bogged down. His first instinct was to go back and match more closely, and although he came out right, he knew his words didn't match his memory of the story. He couldn't remember how it went, but for his own sense of closure he wanted a more accurate match. When rereading didn't work, he didn't know what to do next. He was aware that words have a specific, assigned identification, but he didn't understand how to get at them when story-memory failed, and he was frustrated.

PERSONAL CHARACTERISTICS

Attitude

Strategy dependent children have learned that reading is fun and satisfying. They are enthusiastic about the content of stories and enjoy reading material they have become familiar with during shared language activities. They are proud of their participation in a valued activity. But their stage of awareness tells them they aren't quite grasping everything they need to in order to "own" texts to the degree they instinctively feel is possible. They are past the emergent stage and are showing signs of frustration because they can't quite "get hold of" the print. They *want* to read.

Personality

There is a difference between the *very small* number of children I would call strategy dependent and those who simply need more time and experience with print. Strategy dependent children are life-loving and enthusiastic, often talented artistically or mechanically, but sometimes distractible and possessed of short attention spans when it comes to activities they find boring. They thrive in a good whole language environment because the rich literacy experiences and related activities delight their imaginations and provide outlets for their need to be actively engaged. But because they are adept at such activities as bike-riding, swimming or climbing, and learn new physical skills quickly, they are impatient and easily frustrated with activities that take more time or that focus on small details.

It is this personal frustration that sets them apart. Children who are the same age and at the same point in their reading development but who are *content* with their own rate of progress would not be included here. Nor are children who are frustrated by external pressures. Strategy dependent children *want* to read but can't quite put the pieces together. Their I-want-it-all-at-once personalities, so used to quick mastery in other activities, are frustrated by a process that seemed so easy when they were in the emergent stage but that seems beyond their reach now that they are aware of the importance of print. These are the children, I suspect, who become overpredictive readers in a phonemic segmentation approach.

Reading Style

These children are still relying primarily on story memory to carry their reading. Their reading is generally quite steady, but they move in and out of word-voice matching, usually using their finger as a guide, and so are beginning to read more slowly and deliberately, a normal stage for all beginning readers. What stands out is the frustration they experience when they *want* a closer match between their predictions and the text but can't use the print to help them.

POSSIBLE CAUSES

Global Attending Behaviors

Children in this category are well tuned to their whole environment but lack attention to small details. They are the first to notice the truck outside the window, the visitor peeking through the door, the spider on the floor. They love the illustrations, the expression and the humor of the material chosen for shared reading, and continue to relish those aspects while the teacher and other children take moments to focus on print details. They prefer drawing to writing and, unless redirected, will use all their writing time for drawing. They love to talk and they talk quickly. They forget to do their jobs or put their lunch boxes away. They lose their pencils. They are quite willing to take care of these little details when they are given some extra support in the form of reminders and strategies that help them remember. It just doesn't come naturally to them. They need a little extra structure to help them handle the other side of life: the "left brain" sorts of activities.

Insufficient Focus on Print

Children must learn to use the graphophonic as well as the semantic and syntactic cueing systems. Some teachers seem to believe that choral reading of lots of stories and poems is all it takes to create a reader, but use of print is an integral part of the process as well. In large classes, or classes where there aren't enough writing and print-focusing activities woven into the program, some children may not tune into the use of print.

When they are ready to break into the early reading stage, they don't have enough print problem-solving tools to support their progress.

FOCUS FOR RECOVERY

Reminder: In my discussion of universal principles (Chapter 3) I included a number of points I consider *vital* for any recovery program. Those points are not repeated here, but please don't forget them!

Modeling

When strategy dependent children get bogged down, I call their attention to initial consonant sounds as cues and model their use, as I did with Ricky in the example. I think it's absolutely necessary to show children how to apply their knowledge in real reading situations.

Universal Principles

When these children are referred for standard educational testing they usually do abominably on the reading tests that require them to sound out lists of words, a skill they have never had to develop in a whole language classroom. They are then immediately put into an intensive phonemic-segmentation approach to "catch them up where they belong."

But these tests do nothing to show what the children *do* know about the reading process—usually a great deal. It's important that the understandings and strategies they have already developed continue to be encouraged and strengthened. They should remain in a whole language environment where all the universal principles are practiced.

Writing

This is probably the single best way to help these children concentrate on letter-sound correspondences. If I have time for nothing else, I coach them through the invented spellings of their stories. Here are some specific suggestions for tuning children in to the use of print details:

Alphabet interest books

Have the children make alphabet books listing their favorite things under initial letters. Toy catalogs and "wish books" are good resources for this.

Cloze

Choose familiar predictable stories, putting a strong consonant at the beginning of each blank (one that wasn't used in the original story) so the children have to attend to that sound in choosing a word. I frequently do this with the whole class, using the overhead projector. As a group, we brainstorm possibilities for the blank.

Fizz and Splutter

The *Story Box* set of books has one book called *Fizz and Splutter,* about a magician who keeps trying to make fireworks, saying:

> "Mutter, mutter Fizz and splutter, I'll make a magic . . ."

But each time he waves his wand he produces a letter of the alphabet and a collection of objects that start with that letter. So he tries again:

> "That's not what I want," said the old, old wizard.
> "I'll make a magic . . ."

and another letter appears. In the end he finally succeeds in making fireworks.

I made up booklets that included the verse portions of each page but left blank space for the letters and pictures, and the children created their own versions of *Fizz and Splutter.*

Tongue twisters

Children love creating tongue twisters, and doing so helps draw their attention to letter-sound correspondences. We start out with one I've written on a sentence strip (initial letter in a contrasting color), reading and enjoying it together. Then we brainstorm all the words we can think of that start with the same sound and create new tongue twisters using combinations of those words. The children pick their favorite to add to their personal tongue-twister book.

Short drills

Once I've done some in-context work with initial consonant correspondences, including tongue twisters, I spend about three minutes at the beginning of each one-to-one session going through a set of five cards on which are written five different consonants. I make sure at least two are letters the children know well in terms of both identification and letter-sound correspondence. The other three they are learning. First the children simply name the letters. Then they identify either the letter sound or the name of an object that starts with the letter, whichever is easier. Once they've learned the major consonants (I exclude *x* and *q*) in this manner, I move to dictation, first by letter name, then by letter sound.

Sight words

When the children have enough sight-word cards, they can sort them according to their initial letters and sounds.

READERS MISTAKEN FOR STRATEGY DEPENDENT

It is natural for very young readers to shift from memory reading to a gradually increasing use of print cues. First print is used to assist memory. Then, as specifics become an automatic part of memory, print becomes a full partner in the interaction that involves prediction or expectation, print sampling and confirmation of expectation. Usually children acquire an awareness of letter-sound correspondences *along with* a store of sight words, the ability to word-voice match and sensitivity to other features of words as cues. Children who are developing normally, mixing story memory with the occasional use of print cues, should simply continue to take part in the normal activities of a whole language classroom. It's when some children are starting to show frustration and impatience because they *want* to use the print but don't know how that we need to provide more specific guidance and some focusing activities, one-to-one if necessary.

ADDITIONAL NOTES

By my definition, strategy dependent readers are beginning early readers in a whole language environment. They are strong users of prediction and confirmation, based on memory, but they have trouble mastering print cues. I never meet this particular problem among children who were introduced to reading through a basal program or phonemic segmentation approach, because these programs focus on graphic display from the beginning.

Some people feel that these children simply need more time, that they will break into reading in due course. I agree, except I think the degree of frustration among this small group is serious enough that they could decide to abandon their effort to learn to read, or could be delayed unnecessarily.

We simply need to keep our eyes open. In contrast to most basal programs, which heavily emphasize the graphophonemic system in the early years, the whole language approach gives equal time to all three cueing systems. But we mustn't neglect the third system in reaction to the slanted focus of basal approaches. Print, after all, is the one cueing system that distinguishes reading from oral language learning.

CHAPTER 5

OVERLOADED
READERS

EXAMPLE: VERONICA

Veronica was in mid grade six when she was referred to me. The
children in her 35 student class were grouped for reading instruction, using a basal program well balanced around thematic
coverage of content-area topics at the upper levels. This
program had been in use for only two years. In the early grades
Veronica had been taught by means of a highly sequenced,
phonemic segmentation approach. Her grade six teacher told
me that Veronica attended well and worked persistently but was
having trouble with her work. She couldn't pinpoint what was
causing the problems.

Veronica lives with her large family in a small, isolated community. Her father is a woodcutter; her mother looks after the
house. They are highly supportive of schooling but lack the
means to provide travel and book experiences for their children.
Veronica enjoyed reading at her independent level and within
her interest range: she frequently came to my resource room
and borrowed from my stock of mystery and science fiction
stories.

The following passage from "Don't Hold Your Breath"
(Courtney, 1980) is written at a high grade five readability level.
It's one of the miscue assessment texts used after completion of
the level Veronica had just finished in class. Vocabulary and
topic (scuba diving) had been covered in the basal texts. This

section deals with the concept of air pressure in relation to water pressure. Veronica read the introductory and remaining parts in the same style, although she began to do less self-correcting toward the end. Her reading was slow, essentially word by word, although she "chunked" phrases most of the time.

For this example I am including both a "longhand" and a "miscue-coded" version of the reading to indicate the nature and sound of it as well as the types of miscues. For an interpretation of the symbols used in the coded version see pages 121-122.

Longhand version

Text	**Veronica**
In class, you learn about breathing underwater. It's not the same as breathing in air. If you are breathing normally underwater from the oxygen tank on your back and you want to come up to the surface, you must not hold your breath. You *must* exhale some air. The air in your lungs takes up less space when you go deeper and more space when you rise. Your lungs don't have room for all of it. You must constantly breathe air out of your lungs as you come up.	In case you learn about breathing underwater, do not . . . It's not the same as breathing in air. If you are breathing normally underwater for the oxygen tank . . . from the oxygen tank, you . . . on your back and you want to come up to the surface, you must not hold your breath. You *must* ex . . . exhale some air. The air in your lungs takes up less pla . . . space when you rise. Your lungs don't have room for all of it. You must . . . containly breath . . . air out of your lungs and you come up . . . as you come up.
In the pool, the instructors watch carefully as you practice doing this alone and in groups. They keep reminding you, "Breathe out! Breathe out! Don't hold your breath!" Soon the practice becomes routine.	In the ploo, the . . . inscanners watch carefully as you . . . practice doing this along . . . practice doing this alone and . . . and in groups. They keep reminding you, "Breathe out! Breathe out! Don't hold your breath!" Soon the practice becomes region . . . rowtain.

Miscue-coded version

In class, you learn about breathing underwater. It's not
[case above "class"; ① after class; © do above "underwater", "not" underlined]

the same as breathing in air. If you are breathing normally

underwater from the oxygen tank on your back and you
[© for above "from"; © you above "on"]

want to come up to the surface, you must not hold your

breath. You *must* exhale some air. The air in your lungs
[ex underlined]

takes up less space when you go deeper and more space
[© plā above "space"; © say above "space"]

when you rise. Your lungs don't have room for all of it.

You must/constantly breathe air out of your lungs as you,
[containly above "constantly"; © and above "as you"]

come up.

In the pool, the instructors watch carefully as you/prac-,
[ploo above "pool"; inscanners above "instructors"; ©]

tice doing this alone and in groups. They keep reminding
[along above "alone"]

you, "Breathe out! Breathe out! Don't hold your breath!"

Soon the practice becomes routine.
[region ... rowtain above "routine"]

Retelling

This is the portion of Veronica's retelling that relates to the
above text:

T: Tell me as much as you can remember about what you read.

V: At the first they were telling how . . . the safety of the scuba diving
and that . . . not to breathe in, to breathe out . . . [Portion deleted
here in which she referred to "underscanners."] And something
about when you get lower you should breathe out more and when
you get higher to breathe . . . to breathe out when you're down
and never to breathe in.

T: What do you think an "underscanner" is?

V: Like a safety person?

T: Tell me again when you should breathe out and when you should
breathe in.

V: You should breathe out when you're on higher water and breathe
out when you're down.

T: Breathe in?

40

V: Breathe out . . . breathe *in.*

T: All right.

V: . . . I mean "*inner*scanner," not "outerscanner."

T: Innerscanner. All right. What do you think they are?

V: People that are helpful, that help.

After this I asked Veronica to read me some passages that follow the mid grade four readers. She read fluently, self-corrected appropriately, knew all the vocabulary and gave retellings that indicated complete understanding. She was also much more relaxed.

DISCUSSION

Veronica's transcript shows that she has considerable strength as a reader: she self-corrects, she continues reading when she can't figure out a word, she tries to use graphophonic cues, maintain flow and use substitution, even if it's a nonsense word. She attaches logical meaning to nonsense words: "inscanners," "innerscanners" and "underscanners" for *instructors,* for example.

Her areas of difficulty are vocabulary, sentence length and comprehension of the main concept. Veronica did not predict *instructor, constantly* and *routine.* These words aren't common to her spoken vocabulary and she hasn't read enough books to have gained a comfortable knowledge of such words from that source.

She also doesn't seem accustomed to long sentences like the second one: her reading of "you" after "oxygen tank" shows she was expecting the main part of the sentence to start at that point. The string of prepositional phrases and the double set of adverbial clauses following the initial *If* were difficult for her. Patchy fluency and the miscue that stopped her flow at the word *from* increased the difficulty of holding such a big chunk together. She had even more difficulty with a 26-word sentence at the end of the passage. But she still worked these sentences through, and her retelling indicated that she got a general feel for what was going on. Dealing with such material isn't out of reach for her. She just needs more practice hearing, reading and understanding such sentences and more experience with vocabulary less common to her background.

I don't think Veronica understood the pressure concept on which the main idea of this passage was based. That concept wasn't given an in-depth explanation in the passage and my questioning during the retelling didn't adequately probe her understanding. She would benefit from conceptual preparation before reading a passage such as this.

PERSONAL CHARACTERISTICS

Attitude

Reading is fun.

Overloaded readers caught early still have a positive attitude toward reading. Veronica liked to read when she could pick her own books, accepting and rejecting freely depending on their difficulty and her interests. Such readers have already experienced some success and know the pleasure books can provide. But those who have been overloaded long enough to lose confidence and morale show signs of pulling away from reading as a pleasurable activity.

Personality

They are well balanced.

The children in this category are conscientious, willing and persistent. They demonstrate a healthy balance between following their own interests and conforming to the limits of society. They want to be comfortably successful but don't have a driving need to be "on top." They get along well in any setting. They tend to be the general all-round "good kids" who can sometimes get lost in the shuffle, especially in large classes.

Reading Style

Their fluency is patchy.

On texts at the same level as they read in class, the fluency of these children is often patchy, word-by-word at times, yet with the potential for fluency showing through when they read several words or a phrase evenly and expressively. Fluency depends on the material: they "suddenly" become comfortably fluent readers when the material they are given is of high interest or has primarily familiar vocabulary. This is an important distinction in sorting overloaded readers from underpredictive and overpredictive readers. The latter two types read nothing fluently: the former is fine when the overload is removed.

They make poor substitutions.

When trying to decipher longer or less common words, these children tend to substitute nonsense words, or words which, although they may have high graphophonic similarity, are inappropriate in terms of meaning. Veronica substituted "containly," for *constantly,* "inscanners" for *instructors* and "region," then "rowtain," for *routine.* Her substitutions were of similar length, sound and letter construction as the text words. She may have been so accustomed to reading words that were unfamiliar to her general spoken and listening vocabulary that she wasn't particularly bothered by her choices. Her double substitution for *routine* shows her awareness of phonics rules, and her interpretation of *innerscanners* shows she was able to attach meaning to unknowns. But her overall difficulties with the passage, conceptually, structurally and in terms of vocabulary and interest, were too much for her to use these skills efficiently.

They have difficulty with sentence length.

Overloaded readers have trouble holding the parts of complex sentences together in their minds to form a larger unit of meaning. Strings of prepositional phrases, subordinate clauses and compound sentences throw them off their pace: they often seem to expect a sentence to end sooner than it does.

Their persistence is mixed with frustration.

Overloaded readers, having had successful experiences with reading, do keep going. They expect reading to make sense and try as well as they can under the circumstances to get something out of the material. They self-correct whenever they can clearly see what went wrong, and try to figure out words, as Veronica did — successfully, with *exhale* and *practice* — in spite of fairly lengthy pauses. But they are frustrated by their inefficiency, by the number of words they don't know and the difficulty of holding meaning together. Although they see a passage through to the end, self-correction and rerun strategies drop off as they get more and more bogged down. Tension and frustration are usually observed through non-verbal indicators such as sighing a lot, kicking the table legs or resting their head on one hand.

POSSIBLE CAUSES

Cummulative Reading Programs

In basal reading series, each level adds new elements and new levels of difficulty: vocabulary load increases, sentences become more and more complex, concepts are more advanced, more non-fiction is added and the quantity of reading required for the same time period is increased. Each text is more difficult than the last. Children who are barely keeping up the pace during the first years start to slip behind, imperceptively at first. There's little chance to catch up because there's no consolidation time or material built into the program. Sometimes there is supplementary reading material for those who "finish first," but average achievers need their time just to get the basic material covered. Since they were working satisfactorily until the material became too difficult, they can manage for some time, riding on inference and guesswork, before their problem is noticed, especially if they are part of a large class as Veronica was.

Inexperience with the Structures of Literature

We others, who have long lost the more subtle of the physical senses, have not even proper terms to express an animal's intercommunications with his surroundings, living or otherwise, and have only the word *smell,* for instance, to include the whole range of delicate thrills which murmur in the nose of the animal night and day, summoning, warning, inciting, repelling. It was one of these mysterious fairy calls from out of the void that suddenly reached Mole in the darkness, making him tingle through and through with its very familiar appeal, even while as yet he could not clearly remember what it was. He stopped dead in his tracks, his nose searching hither and thither in its efforts to recapture the fine filament, the telegraphic current, that had so strongly moved him. A moment, and he had caught it again; and with it this time came recollection in fullest flood.

Home!

From *The Wind in the Willows* by Kenneth Grahame

When we speak, we are on familiar ground with our speaking partners, we adjust our dialect to the situation and we supplement our words with gestures and intonation. Sentence length is often controlled by the amount of breath we have. If we want to say something lengthy, we draw our breath at appropriate phrase breaks, a practice that incidentally helps the listener follow our speech. We sometimes stop a speaker and ask for clarification.

But when we *read* long sentences, as in the lyrical passage above, we don't have those extra cues or opportunitites for direct feedback to help us maintain comprehension. We have to help ourselves by relying on punctuation and grammatical structures. We have to carry things like modifying phrases, gerunds, and subordinate clauses in our minds and attach their meanings to the main clause properly. This not only takes practice in reading, it takes practice in listening. Children who haven't had extensive exposure to the writings of authors like E.B. White, William Steig, Roald Dahl and Kenneth Grahame during the first part of their youth will not have developed the capacity to hold long strings of words and parts of thoughts together. Overloaded readers who have trouble with long sentences often haven't had enough experience with the "language of literacy" or "book language." Veronica, for example, may never have heard the expression "to become routine." Even if she had read *routine* correctly, she may not have understood the phrase.

The problem of inexperience is compounded by the use of strangled texts in the early part of many basal programs, which limit text to three- and four-word sentences that never exceed the width of the page and that *always* have the subject precede the predicate. Each time more complex sentences are added into the reading material, new constructions will have to be deliberately pointed out and taught.

Limited Background Experience

Even proficient speakers of English can't always read everything written in the language. Sufficient background knowledge of the concepts, basic vocabulary and "modified" vocabulary (jargon) of the subject matter is essential to understanding a text. Although I can read every word in the advertisement below, I don't have much idea what it's about. The word *corrugating* provides a clue, but what is being corrugated? Metal? Paper? Plastic? And nothing in the entire passage tells me what, precisely, a *flute* is. But I'm sure the manager of the box company where I found the journal that contained the ad would be insulted if it defined the term for him.

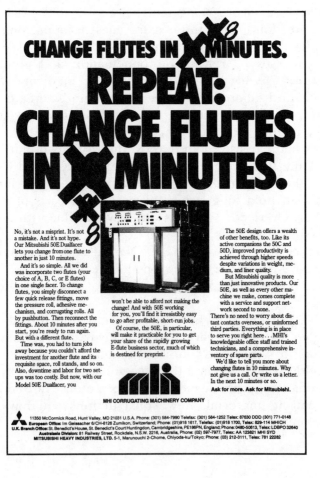

Overloaded readers often don't have sufficient background experience to understand the material they are being asked to read. Either the *subject* or the *concepts* are too unfamiliar for them to make sense of the text. Although Veronica had read a story about scuba divers and had, doubtless, seen Jacques Cousteau on TV, she didn't understand the scientific principles of pressure, particularly the effect of water pressure on air. And without having grasped that concept, she couldn't understand the main idea of the text.

Underdeveloped Sight-Word Vocabulary

Younger overloaded readers may also suffer from a lack of automaticity with the basic four or five hundred words needed to hold text together. On the whole, Veronica's basic sight vocabulary is in pretty good shape, but her miscues on the words *space* and *alone* indicate some lingering problems.

Unfamiliar Vocabulary

I once saw a video from a reading clinic showing a child sounding out lists of words. She got stumped on *amber* because she didn't know where to divide it, or where to put the accent. The teacher corrected her attempt at pronunciation and then asked, "Do you know that word *amber*?" The girl shook her head. Then the teacher said, "That's not a word we see too often, is it?" *And she went on to the next word without defining it!*

It's not true that children like Veronica can't get words simply because they haven't learned their syllabication skills properly. It's useless to sound out a word correctly if the sounds remain meaningless. The vocabulary base of literate people comes from extensive reading and from living with people who have broad spoken vocabularies. The concept of a word's meaning grows out of repeated exposure to that word in a variety of contexts, both heard and read. How often are we asked to define a word but can't unless we are given a context that will trigger our general sense of the word's meaning? Children who are overloaded by vocabulary haven't had enough experience with a broad variety of words to predict automatically those not found in their daily language.

FOCUS FOR RECOVERY

Reminder: In my discussion of universal principles (Chapter 3) I included a number of points I consider *vital* for any recovery program. Those points are not repeated here, but please don't forget them! Fortunately, overloaded readers are the easiest to help with common-sense measures.

Background Knowledge

It is vitally important that children already understand the concepts important to the comprehension of a text before trying to read it. Before Veronica read the scuba diving passage she needed to understand the air/water pressure concept. If I had demonstrated the concept using a filled aquarium and a balloon, and perhaps set up some other experiments for her to carry out herself, she would probably have been more sure in her retelling. I could have introduced the passage by saying, "This passage is about the concept we've been working with, only this time you'll see how it works with the human body." Basal programs sometimes make unwarranted assumptions about children's background knowledge. Teachers need to find out what the children know, through prereading discussions, and provide the necessary experiences before the reading begins.

Experience with Complex Structures

Readers who are having trouble with longer sentences and more complex grammatical structures need to hear and use those structures. Choral reading is an attractive way of doing that. It's active and low risk. It doesn't have to be a babyish activity if the material is properly chosen and purposes are appropriate for the age and interest level. Using poems, chants, poetic prose, even popular songs that contain inverted sentences, long strings of words and phrases, or just interesting turns of phrase, the children first experience, then discuss and try creating for themselves longer, livelier language. There are also some books in enlarged format that children of any age enjoy. Mercer Mayer's *What Do You Do With a Kangaroo?*, Joanne Oppenheim's *Have You Seen Birds?*, Mary Ann Hoberman's *A House Is a House for Me*, and Orin Cochrane's *The Great Gray Owl* all have content of interest and enjoyment for any age, and grammatical structures that are useful for this sort of experience.

Expository Texts

Basal programs don't often provide much experience with non-fiction material before the middle to upper grades. Reading expository text requires its own kind of logic and organization. Fiction uses a start-to-finish, beginning-middle-end structure, while non-fiction is organized in a logical arrangement that depends on the purpose for which it was written and the nature of the information itself. It isn't always read start-to-finish, nor is it always read in its entirety. Readers have to determine the organizational framework being used and carry that framework in mind while reading, so they can make sense of the information they encounter in the text.

Children who haven't read much non-fiction need to be shown how various kinds of material are arranged. The easiest way to do this is to give them experience *writing* a variety of expository texts themselves. To begin the process of understanding different organizational structures, I use matrices, an idea I picked up in a workshop given by a Nova Scotia teacher, Margaret Crocker. More formal outlines are introduced later.

Shown below and on the next page are some organizational structures appropriate for several kinds of expository material.

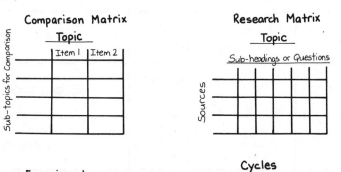

Formal Outline	News Articles
I. Main Topic	Who ?
A. Sub-topic	What ?
B. Sub-topic	Where?
II. Main Topic	When?
A. Sub-topic	Why ?
B. Sub-topic	How ?
C. Sub-topic	

The chart below shows how a matrix can be filled in. Once it has been completed with information gathered from source material, the children write their reports simply by fleshing out the facts in paragraph form under each heading. While they are working on writing, they are also digesting the writing they read to produce the reports, on their own and in class teaching groups.

	Ringtail Cat	Raccoon Dog
Relatives	raccoons	foxes
Food	fruit, nuts, small animals, insects	←——— same
Location	North and Central America	Asia and Europe
Appearance	ringed tail like a raccoon, grey-brown, short, fine fur.	masked like a raccoon. greyish, bushy fur.
Habits	nocturnal, rests in caves, hollow trees, rock crevices.	nocturnal, dens in ground holes, hollow logs, caves, rock crevices.

Individualized Reading

Whole language teachers use a wide range and variety of reading materials for children to choose from, and consider the basals a resource and general guide for teaching specific skills. Lessons are tailored more to individual needs than to published programs. Small-group conferences centered around thematic reading, or around a particular story that several children have read, help the teacher to recognize when certain children are having trouble with more difficult text, and to determine when to organize teaching groups around some of the suggestions in this section.

Readjusted Expectations

The label itself suggests the best "cure" for overloaded readers: eliminate unreasonable expectations. If a basal program continues to be mandatory, have the children work in another series, at a parallel instructional level, and so avoid repetition of material already read. Or continue with the existing basal but slow down the pace and spend more time with preparatory activities, supplementary projects and discussions that will provide experience with the vocabulary and set the concepts.

Ideally, most of the children's reading time should be spent with self-selected material. The majority will regulate their own level of challenge and growth. Of course there are some who need a push and others who pressure themselves too much. Our job is to watch and make appropriately timed interventions that will maintain a balance between growth and consolidation, based on individual learning styles. New strategies for efficient handling of print are introduced as the children show signs they are ready to absorb them.

Sight-Word Recognition

See pages 19-21.

Writing

See pages 27-29.

CHAPTER 6

UNDERPREDICTIVE READERS

EXAMPLE: JASON

I was a reading resource teacher when Jason was sent to me in the middle of his grade three year. He was very quiet, reserved and tense. He didn't look at me. When I asked him to read one of the more recent stories he had read in class he chose "The Three Billy Goats Gruff" from his reader. Without glancing at the illustrations, he began reading immediately.

"Ay [long *a*] . . . long . . . time . . . ay . . . ag . . . ay'go . . . three . . . bill . . . bill . . . y . . . goat . . . live [long *i*] . . . lived [still long *i*] . . . in . . . ay . . . v . . . v . . . v . . . awl . . . vawl . . ."

Here Jason came to a halt. He tried a few more times to get *valley*, without success, and then proceeded to stare at the word, holding his finger under it in the book. I waited for about two minutes. He didn't budge.

"What are you having trouble with?" I asked.

"I can't get that word."

"Would you like to keep going for now?"

Almost zombie-like, his finger moved under the next word.

"They . . . aaa [short *a*] . . . teee . . . gr . . . grrrr . . . aa . . . ss . . . grass . . . all . . . day . . . l . . . lone."

Enough, of course. I suggested some other stories. But even when I gave him material at a primer level his approach remained the same: he read word by word, and the only strategy he would allow himself to use for dealing with unknown words was blending. Comprehension was limited to latching on to a few words or phrases, with no idea of what a story was all about.

EXAMPLE: LINDA

In the spring my own 20 first-graders are joined for a morning by the new candidates for fall entrance into grade two, so the school and the children can become better acquainted. One of my tasks is to assess their reading achievements. The best I can do is listen to each visitor read for three or four minutes, often while I'm doing something else. Linda was such a visitor.

"Tell me a bit about your reading," I started, trying to leave the query as open-ended as possible.

"Well, I can read *some* books," she said. She looked a bit anxious as she said this, as though she hoped I wouldn't pin her down.

"What are some stories you've read?" I asked.

Her eye traveled around the room and focused on my enlarged-print version of *The Gingerbread Man* sitting on the reading board.

"Oh! That's *The Gingerbread Man!* I've read that! But ours was different than that one," she added hastily.

"That's a favorite here just now. Do you like the story?"

"Yup."

"Great!" I said. "I have that story in this book here. Why don't you sit on that chair and read to me for a few minutes while I pin up these pictures?"

I handed her a book that contained a different version of the story than the one on the rack, simply written but not contrived. Suddenly she looked very nervous.

"Oh," she said, "but this isn't the one I know. I haven't had this one. I might not know how to read this." The anxiety level indicator was on red.

"Well, you know what happens in the story, right?"

Tentatively, "Yeah . . ."

"How about just giving it a try and I'll help you if you need it."

"Ummm, well, O.K." Still tentative, but somewhat reassured.

I made myself very busy and didn't go near Linda or look in her direction, though I observed peripherally in passing. She perched herself tensely on a stool and studied the page intently. Her shoulders were hunched, her arms tight against her body. She had her finger under the first word and I could hear her making sounds.

"Ohhhh . . . ohhh . . . ennnn . . . ohh . . . ennn . . . kkkk. Aw . . . aw . . . awnnnkkeee."

This went on for a while, then silence. I said, "How are you doing?" as I continued putting up a bulletin board.

"I can't get this word," she said. "I haven't had this one before."

"Oh. Well, how about reading me the ones you do know then?"

She looked slightly alarmed. "You mean skip this one?"

"Try it," I said.

She stared at me for a moment, then looked down at the page. Her finger moved on to the next word.

"Uh . . . up . . . *up!!* . . . up . . . on. Up . . . on? Up on? *Upon!* Upon?" She looked up at me expectantly after this last query. I glanced over my shoulder, smiled and said, "Keep going!" Relief flooded her face.

"Upon . . . a . . . time. Upon a ti . . . *Oh!* Once upon a time!" She rushed the words out in a blast of triumph. Then concern swept over her and she looked up at me again. "Is that right?" she asked.

"Do you think a story might start out that way?" I asked in return. "Does it make sense?"

"Yeeeesss," she said carefully, with just an edge of defensiveness.

"Well then?"

She looked a bit surprised, a bit confused. "Shall I read some more?"

"Sure," I said, with my back turned.

Linda continued reading one word at a time, sounding out each word she didn't know automatically and seeking my approval. After a while she got used to the fact that I wasn't going to approve or disapprove her choices and the questioning tone disappeared when she made predictions. Although she continued to use the blending procedure as her choice in confronting new words, she strangled each word less and less as I encouraged her to "keep going." Her reading was ponderously slow and patchy, but the potential for improvement began to show by the time she was halfway through the story.

DISCUSSION

Jason and Linda are both underpredictive readers. Underpredictive readers don't use what they already know about language, the story, the pictures, or life in general to help them predict. They consider only the text itself at its most superficial, visual level. They believe that reading is a difficult and exacting task, that they must read every word precisely as it is on the page and that they must decode a word from left to right, letter by letter. Above all, they don't see themselves as initiators or controllers of the reading process who may proceed without approval. They believe it's wrong to guess. They are always checking over their shoulder with the nearby adult to see if they are "doing it right." And they don't consider the task complete until they've been told by someone else that they are finished. They are dependent and may end up as total non-readers outside of school.

Jason was a high-risk candidate for becoming a functionally illiterate adult. He was so teacher-dependent that when I offered a solution to him he responded like an automaton. There was no sense of revelation or surprise, no attempt to construct meaning: the teacher said "Do this" and he did it. Period. He was nearly at a standstill.

Linda was much less damaged and would be able to recover quickly given the right priming and encouragement. She responded with delight at the recognition of a meaningful phrase when she finally put "Once upon a time" together. Cautious as she was, she was willing to try to make meaning and was beginning to see the connection between prediction and reading. The longer I left her alone, the more independent she became.

PERSONAL CHARACTERISTICS

Attitude

Reading has no intrinsic purpose.

Underpredictive readers don't understand that the basic purpose for reading is to gain meaning from text. They only see a task to be performed on command in a systematic, rule-bound sequence. They do as they are told in order to avoid consequences they fear will be more unpleasant than the task itself. They can't consider the goal of taking possession of the process for themselves and producing the magic that fluent readers create from text.

Reading is painful.

Underpredictive readers read little, if any, for personal pleasure. The difficulties of getting through even a short passage produce no personal satisfaction, no sense of revelation or discovery. They read only when required, avoiding the process as much as possible. Some won't even look at picture books when choice-reading is allowed.

Personality

They are fearful and lack confidence.

"I can't read" is frequently the first pronouncement underpredictive readers make at our initial meeting. They don't *see* themselves as readers, or even potential readers. They don't give themselves credit for what they *can* do. Risk-taking is almost non-existent: they don't want to try anything they aren't completely sure of, believing, as Linda did, that they can't read any word that hasn't been directly taught. I frequently see nervous behaviors while underpredictive readers are reading — foot-tapping or rhythmic kicking of a table leg, constant shifting as though they are uncomfortable, nervous movements of their hands. Two children would actually cringe if I made an unexpected move.

They are highly conscientious.

In my experience, underpredictive readers try very hard to please. They are often plodders who are bothered when they can't finish all their assigned work. They regularly check with the teacher. They work so diligently to apply the lessons and rules they've been taught that they actually stop themselves from using intuitive strategies that might tempt them. Because they don't carry meaning *with* them as they read, they don't combine meaning-getting strategies with the use of surface graphophonic and word analysis skills. Their very conscientiousness prevents them from going beyond what they've been taught.

Reading Style

Their fluency is patchy.

Underpredictive readers read in an uneven, word-by-word fashion. They may read several words in a row fairly smoothly, but as soon as they come to one that causes them the slightest doubt they stop and begin their "attack" on it. Their decoding almost always begins with the initial letter and moves progressively along the word. They rarely allow their eye to glance at other available clues: the ending of the word, succeeding words, pictures. If their eyes should stray, they do so furtively. These readers work over individual words, trying combinations of sounds that correspond to the letters they see. Some children, like Jason, will remain focused on a single word until an outsider helps them. Most, however, will eventually settle for any word or word-like utterance that more or less fits the visual cues, and move on. We get a highly choppy, tedious, meaningless collection of grunts and groans sprinkled with real words and phrases. It's deathly to listen to.

Decoding is their sole strategy.

Underpredictive readers have been led to believe that reading is a letter-by-letter puzzle-solving activity. They know no other skill or strategy. These children have as much knowledge of language as any, but they forbid themselves to apply that knowledge because they have the notion that doing so would be cheating. If they have not applied the phonics rules they've been taught, they have not read. Reading, for these children, is a maze to be negotiated.

They are over-dependent on authority figures.

These readers are face-watchers. They are acutely tuned to the teacher's non-verbal responses—frowns, looks of doubt or expectation, body tension, etc. Some children look up at me after nearly every word, ending each time with a questioning intonation. Others never look at me, but I'm conscious that their peripheral vision is constantly alert, evidenced by an immediate reaction to my slightest shift. "Reader's block" occurs when they come to a word they can't handle, and they are afraid or unwilling to go on. If they feel they are being monitored, they don't take risks.

When I was new at resource work and believed I shouldn't intervene no matter how long the child waited, one sixth-grade 13-year-old boy waited me out *four minutes,* measured later from the tape recording. He won. I did finally suggest that he skip the word and go on.

They show little comprehension.

Because it takes these readers so long to work out each word, they forget what they've already read. Their comprehension is as patchy as their oral reading: they latch onto words and phrases and try to put together something from the bits and pieces, or they simply say they don't remember what happened.

POSSIBLE CAUSES

Early Fragmentation of Print

Many reading programs initiate reading instruction by focusing heavily on very small units of text—individual letters, groups of letters such as blends, and forms like contractions and variant endings that are really spelling skills more than reading skills. Children who haven't entered school with a strong book orientation, and for whom reading period always begins with a lesson focusing on a letter or structural analysis skill, learn to define reading as the activity of examining various *parts* of words. The sight of text automatically gears them up to start looking at bits and pieces rather than thinking of what the author may have intended to say. Children who understand what reading is for — the making of meaning — are able to extend their thinking beyond this singular focus and use the graphophonic and structural analysis skills as only two of many interlocking parts of the process.

Heavily Monitored Reading

Some of the most seriously underpredictive readers come from the classrooms of the most conscientious and organized teachers. These caring people want to make sure the children learn everything they teach. When everyone else is quietly and gainfully occupied, they work in a concentrated manner with one small group. Most of the "official" reading is done orally, with the teacher free to listen carefully. Every smallest mistake is caught and corrected on the spot, on the theory that wrong habits caught early will not become set. But the unwanted result is that susceptible children learn to risk only the two practices that don't result in public correction: reading automatically recognized words and sounding out others.

Personality

These readers often seem to be exceptionally obedient, well-behaved children who do as they are told and maintain a low profile to avoid upsetting the teacher. If the teacher says decoding is the way, then they will decode, decode and nothing but decode.

Precision Reading

Underpredictive readers have been taught that reading is a very precise, exacting process. They believe that there is only one right choice and that omissions, additions and substitutions meaningful to the context are *wrong*. Every syllable of every word must be carefully accounted for. "Take a closer look" is the admonition they are used to, and they know they will get corrected every time they try any of the less precise strategies so successfully practiced by efficient readers.

FOCUS FOR RECOVERY

Reminder: In my discussion of universal principles (Chapter 3) I included a number of points I consider *vital* for any recovery program. Those points are not repeated here, but please don't forget them! The glossary also contains information useful for planning recovery work.

Appropriate Materials

See page 19.

I choose the most predictable materials available in the beginning stages: books that are well illustrated, fun, easy to learn and easy to adapt. Above all, they should not be contrived, with vocabulary limited to words that will obey the "rules." I look for stories in which general ideas are more important than specific details. For example, Mercer Mayer's *Just for You* focuses on the *idea* of doing something for someone, whereas a book of simple science experiments, although predictable in format, would require precise attention to detail. Underpredictive readers need to concentrate on the big picture, on ideas and overall meanings.

Each time I think we're ready to move on, I offer a small selection of both new and familiar books I think will be easy and interesting and let the children choose which one they would like to learn to read. Choice is important for giving children a personal investment in "possessing" the text for themselves.

Cloze

See page 22.

Oral cloze exercises for underpredictive readers should emphasize *prediction* in their structure. Since these children don't make use of previous content or personal background knowledge, I select or write cloze passages in which what *precedes* the blank provides strong clues for predicting a meaningful insert. At first the choices should be obvious and easy — suitable nouns and action verbs — and any word that maintains the meaning of the text should be accepted. In order to de-emphasize the focus on print details, I don't provide word choices for the blanks when I first work with these children, but encourage them to pick their own words. As reading facility develops, however, I start adding initial consonants or blends at the beginning of the blanks, although I still accept anything meaningful.

Confidence

See pages 16-17.

Elimination of Phonics

Over-phonication is at the root of the troubles of underpredictive readers. Particularly for some of the most common words, often those that introduce a sentence (*there, who, come, the,* etc.), the application of phonics rules fail the children more often than not in the beginning stages of learning to read. Because these readers have the notion that reading is strictly a left-to-right procedure, they always attack words letter by letter from left to right. That's why a word like *mother* can come out "mot-heer." Not only have they not learned to use context (*mother* usually has plenty of context to support it), but they don't realize they can "chunk" various parts of a word (the *-er* ending or the *th* in the middle) to provide themselves with more reliable graphophonic clues. They don't look for word family associations, which also involves looking at the endings of words. They are like a train on a track: there is only one direction—forward. They desperately need to strengthen other reading strategies and put phonics back into its proper place: a final rather than a first resort.

I *never* ask underpredictive readers to sound out a word or to apply a phonics rule, even if I know they know the rule well. I always steer them toward an appropriate meaning-getting strategy by saying something like, "What would make sense there?" or "Try reading ahead for more clues." Only when confidence and strategies are well built up do I incidentally note word families as they occur in the rhymes the children find in the predictable materials they are reading. If a child says, "Hey, those two words rhyme!" I might follow up with, "Yes. And look, they're spelled almost the same way too!" as I point out visual similarity. We make adaptations of favorite rhyming stories or poems and brainstorm new rhyming words to fill in the blanks. We leave the rules alone.

Enjoyment

See pages 17-18.

Experience of Fluency

Underpredictive readers don't know what fluency is. They may *hear* fluent readers, particularly the teacher, but they have never *experienced* fluent reading themselves. They don't know what it feels like to read fluently. Using supported reading techniques and materials limited to their independent level for a time are the best ways I've found to improve fluency. Language experience stories also help.

Ownership

See pages 18-19.

Sequencing Activities

Since underpredictive readers are overly focused on details, I have them sequence chunks of text. I take a copy of a whole story and cut it apart in pages or other logical segments and have the children reconstruct the story meaningfully. It's particularly useful to pick stories that can be restructured in a number of ways and still make sense. For example, a version of *The Three Little Pigs* that doesn't specify whether the house of straw or the house of sticks is built first can be reassembled either way. Variations help these children become less rigid in their outlook on reading. I prefer doing sequencing activities with a group rather than one-to-one because of the discussions that can be generated about meaning.

Sight-Word Recognition

See pages 19-21.

Sight-word building is a universal principle of reading. Nevertheless, I make it only a small part of my work with underpredictive readers until they have developed other strategies more fully. They are too detail-bound already. It's better to promote sight-word building at first just by choosing books that use specific words in abundance. I don't do much card work until confidence and fluency are built up.

Strategies

See pages 21-24. Underpredictive readers need practice developing all strategies, *particularly* those that encourage prediction.

Supported Reading

See pages 24-27. This is a mainstay of the recovery program for these readers!

Writing

See pages 27-29.

READERS MISTAKEN FOR UNDERPREDICTIVE

There are two situations in which a child's surface reading may appear to indicate an underpredictive reader.

Deliberate Readers

Occasionally I come across readers who are so tediously slow that I can't imagine how they will ever get through, never mind remembering anything about the story. On the surface such children sound very much like underpredictive readers, but there are four differences that indicate theirs is a reading *style* rather than a reading problem.

They read steadily and persistently.

Taped recordings of deliberate readers reveal that, although their rate of reading is very slow, it is also very steady. Underpredictive readers stop-start and wait for long periods of time, but these children keep going. They don't wait for the teacher; they work things out for themselves. They also seem inexhaustible. They never stop to complain about the length of a piece but willingly finish whatever they've been asked to read.

They frequently self-correct.

Deliberate readers may make many miscues, but they almost always correct themselves with a high degree of accuracy in terms of both meaning and graphophonic accuracy.

They show detailed comprehension.

Perhaps most remarkable is that, during retelling, these readers show excellent comprehension of the material they read. They retain large quantities of minute detail, as well as a thorough and thoughtful understanding of the overall concepts. (This underscores the importance of the retelling portion of an assessment session. Many standardized reading tests consist only of word lists. Such a test has nothing to do with *reading:* a child could sound out a word perfectly without having any idea what it means. The child's response to a passage after reading is the only real way of knowing how well he or she read.)

Their speech is slow.

Deliberate readers are often also deliberate talkers. They need time to get their ideas out because they speak in such a slow, drawn-out way. They are the ones for whom I turn on the "extra patience" switch in my brain. Their ideas are well thought out and clearly presented — but oh *my,* does it take a while to hear them through!

Normal Phase-Two Oral Readers

In the process of becoming independent readers children go through several phases of oral reading behavior. The first is highly fluent, memory-based reading where cues are taken from pictures, page sequences and overall memory of the pattern of the story. As children become more aware that print carries the message, they begin to focus on specific words. Fully into this phase, many children slow down to a word-by-word crawl, with frequent stoppings and stumblings as they struggle to reconcile print cues with their memory of the story.

But children who are going through this phase in a *healthy* way don't spend excessive time on unknown words. They push themselves to keep reading, and question meaning frequently with comments like, "What? That doesn't make sense!" They often self-correct and, although they ask for help when they're really stumped, they don't depend on others any more than they have to. Close observation of their reading shows that they don't rely on any one skill or strategy but run through a gamut of approaches until they've made enough meaning to satisfy themselves. They see reading as a rewarding challenge they are bound and determined to master. They are confident and proud of themselves: they see themselves as competent.

ADDITIONAL NOTES

Efficient readers constantly anticipate what the text will communicate, using general background knowledge, the purpose they have set for themselves in reading, specific observations of the text itself, and knowledge of the structure of language.

For example, I may be given a book by someone I know loves science fiction novels about human colonies on other planets. Before I've even looked at the title I can predict that the book is not about fly fishing or dog grooming. The cover shows two red suns shining hotly over a broad expanse of sand dunes, and my previous prediction is refined to anticipate a story set in a relatively harsh, waterless world. Further predictions flow around my knowledge of deserts: the wildlife, conditions, clothing and lifestyles that I have experienced or learned about during my lifetime. If there were no book jacket, only the title *Dune* for a clue, my predictions would probably be broader, including my experiences with coastlines of the Americas as possible settings. The fewer the clues, the broader the range of possibilities.

When it comes to the actual text, knowledge of the grammatical structure of language helps to narrow our range of predictions considerably. We know there are only so many alternatives that fit in a given grammatical setting. For example, if a sentence begins *The man had lost* _____ , we aren't likely to predict a verb for the next word; a preposition, adjective, article, adverb or noun are all possible. The context beyond the blank further narrows sensible possibilities. If the sentence reads *The man had lost* _____ *to his opponent,* where the blank represents a single word, then a preposition, article or adjective will have to be ruled out as nonsensical. Only a noun (*ground, money, points,* etc.) or adverb (*badly, quickly, poorly, out,* etc.) makes sense.

But we don't think through the prediction process in this analytical manner when we read. We make our predictions almost instantly. As long as they make sense when matched against our perception of the textual clues, we continue. When we lose sense, we go back and re-examine the text to see where we, or the author, got off track.

Underpredictive readers don't trust themselves to make predictions or judgments. They are so literal in their approach to text that they've ruled their knowledge of language out of the process. Prediction is the gas that drives the reading process, and a reader low on gas stutters and stumbles and soon comes to a complete stop. Underpredictive readers need to be encouraged to use their knowledge of language, their background knowledge and their opinions and observations — their "world view" — to help them read. They need to understand that their tank is full, that they just need to unclog the carburetor!

CHAPTER 7

OVERPREDICTIVE READERS

EXAMPLE: CASEY

Casey is a cheerful, willing, chatty, mildly distractible girl who was referred to me for assessment in the middle of grade two because she was having trouble with comprehension exercises. I asked her to read a passage designed to follow the reader she had just finished. It was at a high grade one readability and contained the vocabulary and concepts she had just been dealing with. She was to do the best she could without my help and would be asked to retell the story when she was finished. The title and pictures provided her with clues. She was comfortable with the procedure and wasn't bothered by the tape recorder.

Casey's father has never been able to read, in spite of repeated tries, yet has tested above average in mechanical ability. Her brother Matt is one of the children sampled for the chapter on global learners. The family lives in abject poverty in a rural area beyond walking distance to any community, even the bookmobile stop. They are very close and supportive of each other.

The following miscue analysis records Casey's reading of a passage from *Evaluation Resource Book for Grade One* (Courtney, 1979).

The Monster of Blue Lake

©It's

It was time to go home.

They're
There's
"Is everyone on the bus?" asked The bus driver.

yes! ©
so...
"Not yet," said Mr. Brown. "Kim and Susan are not

here."

Came
Just then, Kim and Susan ran up to the bus. "Come
mother
and see what we found," they cried. "There is a monster

in Blue Lake."

This is mother the
Mr. Brown said, "There are no monsters in Blue Lake.
This
Maybe you saw a big fish jump out of the water."

mother With
"No, no," said Kim. "It was a monster. We saw its
tail...teeth her mouth
tracks in the sand."

Mr. Brown said, "O.K. Let's go to the lake and see."
out of
Everyone got off the bus and ran to the lake.
Look [yawn] the
Joe took the camera. He wanted to get a good picture
© fff...
of the monster.

Some ★
"Look," said Susan, "here are the monster's big
tail ★ monster's ... no,
tracks." © mother's
th... look toe
Joe took a picture of the tracks.
Let began T mother came
"Let's get out of here before the monster comes,"
Jill "Come on," said Jill ^
said Jack. "Come on," said Jack

all hand
Just then, there was a big splash.

It
"It's the monster," cried Kim. "And it's coming out of

the water."

68

Everyone looked at the water. First they saw the *Fish were seen*
monster's head. Then they saw the monster's hands. *hand (AC)*

Jill laughed. "It's not a monster," she said. "It's a man.
It just looks like a monster." "Is that the end of it?" *joking.*

Then everyone laughed. *Joke*
Joe asked, "May I take your picture, Mr. Monster?" *our*

"O.K." said the man.

"I want to be in the picture with the monster, too," said
Susan.
"Me too," said Jack. *and the and*

Joe took three pictures. *Take*

On the way back home, Mr. Brown made up a funny *jumped*
song about the monster for everyone to sing. The song *began   see*
was called The Monster of Blue Lake.

Retelling

T: O.K. Now tell me that story.

C: There was a monster . . . well, first Kim and Jill saw the monster .
. . uh, well, they saw something in the lake so they run up to the
bus and they tell Mr. Brown about it. And . . . um, so . . . uh, they
all run down to the lake and all of a sudden they took a picture of
a footprint. Then they saw a hand come out. Then they saw two
hands come out of the water. Then they said it was a monster so
they all st . . . first Jill started laughing, then all of them started
laughing. Then they took pictures of Jill, Jack and the monster.

T: Tell me more about the monster.

C: The monster? Um . . . it had long fingers . . . and it had slime in
its hand . . . and, uh . . . it was a man.

T: It was a man. O.K. Tell me more about taking the pictures.

C: Well, when they took the picture it flashed and the man's head
could have popped out . . . out of the costume.

T: Oh, I see. [I didn't!] Tell me more about just before they ran down to the lake after Susan and Kim . . .

C: Went up?

T: . . . came to tell them they had seen the monster [trying to probe her understanding of Mr. Brown's response].

C: Um . . . they saw a great big footprint and then they looked in the water and they seen funny things going on in the water.

T: How did some of the children feel?

C: Um . . . scared, and some felt silly.

T: How do you know that some felt scared?

C: 'Cause . . . well, Jill . . . no, Kim was going like this [gesture like dark-haired girl in the picture] and um . . . and Susan was going wooo-wooo like that [scared-mouth gesture, like the picture] and Jill was laughing.

T: And Jill was laughing. O.K. How did Mr. Brown feel about there being monsters in the lake?

C: [with a shrug] I don't know.

T: Where were the other children when Kim and Susan came to tell them?

C: They were all in the bus, piled in the bus.

T: Why were they in the bus?

C: To go home.

T: After they took pictures of the monster, what happened?

C: The monster wanted to come back with them . . .

T: O.K.

C: . . . and Mr. Brown said he could.

T: O.K. Then what happened.

C: Um . . . took them on the bus and then he went home. And Mr. Brown showed all the pictures of them . . . on the bus.

DISCUSSION

An arm's-length inspection of Casey's reading reveals that the most outstanding features are large numbers of substitutions and omissions and a lack of self-correction. If meaning is maintained, neither of these is necessarily a problem. With fourth-stage oral readers, uncorrected meaning-loss miscues are common and acceptable if the retelling shows good comprehension.

But closer inspection shows that most of Casey's miscues are of poor quality. Her retelling has the gist of the story but her accuracy with details is patchy at best. Many of her inferences come from the pictures rather than the text (the children's reactions, the slime on their hands, the footprints in the sand), and she freely makes up story parts both during her reading and in the retelling. Her yawn halfway through and her willingness to neglect meaning in favor of getting through quickly are evidences that Casey isn't terribly interested in reading. She simply doesn't get enough out of it to make it a worthwhile activity. On the other hand, she has a good beginning bank of sight words, has a natural tendency to chunk for fluency, is capable of self-correcting, can use word-family associations *(took/look)* and initial consonant cues, and does make meaning, even if it's chiefly her own.

PERSONAL CHARACTERISTICS

Attitude

Reading is someone else's bag.

Overpredictive readers see reading as a teacher task that really hasn't much to do with their personal interests. They don't see books as a source of pleasure or information. They don't grasp the concept of being able to understand an author through text. They don't believe that reading, as a process, is something they might want to do. For them, all that's necessary is to get enough out of the text to satisfy the teacher's minimum expectations for the follow-up exercises so they can still go out for recess.

Reading is like spinach — eat it quickly and then savor the good stuff!

Overpredictive readers see reading as a race to be won: get through and get on with life! It's easy to spot overpredictive readers during the administration of a standardized reading test. They usually finish before anyone else and happily but discreetly occupy themselves with the toys and trinkets stored in their desks while everyone else is slaving away. My observations suggest that they don't bother to read the passage: they simply fill in the blanks and circle at random. The correlation between my observations and my own assessments, done through miscue analysis, have led me, finally, to see some value in standardized tests!

Personality

They are action oriented.

Happy-go-lucky, cheerful, willing, dreamy, artistic, mechanical, playful, talkative, casual and selectively distractible are all terms I've heard applied to the overpredictive children I've worked with. They seem very much involved in life, have strong interests outside school and enjoy the more dramatic or choice-oriented in-school activities. They have no use for activities that are boring or nonsensical or that seem to have no immediate purpose. They aren't strongly influenced by the usual kinds of school consequences: threats, cajoling or conscience-plays. They like positive consequences: freedom, privileges, discoveries, purposeful and interesting projects, humorous outcomes.

Reading Style

Their accuracy is poor.

Word recognition, sentence-level meaning and comprehension all suffer because of the lack of self-correction that is characteristic of overpredictive readers. Omissions, substitutions and insertions are frequent, and intonation is thrown off by inattention to punctuation and inappropriate phrase chunking.

Their fluency is inconsistent.

Overpredictive readers are sometimes overlooked longer than other types of troubled readers. They can sound fairly fluent when they read aloud because they don't stop for each word: they keep going, making up their own "sense" or just sampling the words they know well while creating a steady flow of nonsense. Also, since they get through more text than slower readers, they can usually get the gist of simple stories and fill in the necessary details by inference. They usually answer the kinds of questions early-level workbooks ask by using common sense and the impressions they've gleaned from their skimming. It's when the demands for comprehension become more complex that these children show they are having trouble. Closer attention proves their fluency is deceptive. Casey was picked up early because she was an extreme case and her fluency was quite patchy.

They overuse graphic clues.

While reading, overpredictive readers tend to use words that start with the same letters as those in the text, or have the same general configuration, but that don't maintain the meaning of the story or the grammatical logic of the sentence. Casey's transcript is full of examples of an overuse of graphic cues at the expense of meaning.

They overuse personal interpretation.

These readers also tend to predict so freely that their anticipations lead them too far away from the author's intent. Although Casey clearly made an internal adjustment by the time she reached the end of the story, her repeated reading of "mother" for *monster* is a single-word example. Her sentence "It was a mother with its tail . . . teeth in her mouth," substituted for *It was a monster. We saw its tracks in the sand* is an example on the paragraph level.

Their comprehension is sketchy.

Because of these reading-style characteristics, overall comprehension is sketchy and based to a considerable extent on inference and personal fabrication. Making inferences and bringing background knowledge to the reading act are desirable only to the extent that the integrity of the story is maintained, however. A high degree of poor accuracy will result in misunderstandings serious enough to distort the purposes for reading. I worked with one boy who loved carrying out magic tricks and science experiments, but because of his overpredictive reading, his tricks and experiments seldom worked for him. His reading wasn't accurate enough to pick up the necessary details.

POSSIBLE CAUSES

Early Fragmentation of Print

Breaking words into parts—letter-sounds and morphemic segments—is the most abstract and difficult of all reading-related activities. It puts a heavy strain on both short- and long-term memory, as well as on analyzing and synthesizing abilities. Not only must children remember letter-sound correspondences; they must also remember the conditions that determine those correspondences. A letter represents one particular sound, if it represents a sound at all, only when the letters and words around it are arranged in certain specific ways. Take the word *the*, for example. When children read that word, they have to remember that *t* doesn't represent a /t/ sound when followed by *h*, that *h* doesn't sound like /h/ when preceded by *t*, that the *e* in this particular word represents a schwa sound (unless, of course, the next word starts with a vowel, in which case it makes the sound of a long *e*) — and that the word has been taught as a sight word and they are supposed to remember it as a morphemic unit of sound anyway! On top of all this mental juggling, they must try to maintain the sense of what they are reading. That's a lot of work for the two or three years of instruction that normally lead to a rate of processing sufficiently fluent for the flow of meaning to help carry the decoding burden. Some children simply aren't suited for this kind of work.

Feelings of Failure

If children don't share the teacher's belief that mastery of reading is a valuable language process, they aren't going to invest in it unless it provides them with on-the-spot gratification. The constant early failure that troubled readers in this category have experienced drives them away from a process without immediate benefit or immediate satisfaction. Reading, for them, becomes a race to be run, with freedom of mind the prize.

Lack of Purpose

Overpredictive readers don't see a need for reading. It isn't in their minds that reading is a desirable process, theirs to "own." The material they've been asked to read is too boring or purposeless to catch their interest. They haven't had the opportunity to experience reading as a joyful, ear-catching, mind-catching activity in which they can participate without difficulty. In my experience, they frequently come from backgrounds that aren't oriented toward school or literary activities, and their teachers didn't take time to establish those orientations before beginning formal reading instruction.

FOCUS FOR RECOVERY

Reminder: In my discussion of universal principles (Chapter 3) I included a number of points I consider *vital* for any recovery program. Those points are not repeated here, but please don't forget them!

Cloze

See page 22.

For overpredictive readers it's important that the words *following* the blank should provide the context for determining what will go in the space. These children don't do enough confirming in their reading, don't stop and self-correct when meaning has been lost, don't try to determine what caused the problem. Cloze exercises that remove a degree of predictability but incorporate confirmation information will help strengthen this strategy.

Confidence

See pages 16-17.

I always start out with material I know the children will be able to read successfully. If they don't have an independent reading level yet, I use supported reading techniques. I spend time talking about content and responses, and compliment whatever processing demonstrates efficiency and strength. I work only *gradually* into more challenging material so I don't risk turning the children off again.

Enjoyment

See pages 17-18.

We have to help these children *want* to read! Because they don't see why they should learn to read, they need to be immersed in literacy activities so interesting, so grabbing that they come to see the value of the activity. They need to see that without reading they won't have access to activities that are important to them.

I use material that contains details or instructions for carrying out a desirable function or activity:

- cooking;
- doing a craft;
- playing a game;
- operating a machine;
- conducting a scientific experiment;
- solving a puzzle;
- enjoying a treasure hunt;
- performing magic tricks.

Such texts provide action-oriented children with activities of high interest and encourage them to attend to the details of print. I start with texts that are accompanied by clear, detailed diagrams, such as origami projects, and gradually move to some that rely only on written directions. (See also pages 18-19.)

Experience of Fluency

Many overpredictive readers have a sense of fluency already. I try to get them to slow down for meaning without losing that sense. The technique described below is the best way I've found for managing the delicate balance.

Meaning

This is my single most successful one-to-one technique for working with overpredictive readers, one that preserves their legitimate prediction tendencies. I ask them to read aloud a passage that is partially familiar or close to their independent level, while I sit somewhere in the room where I can't see the text. I tell them I'll stop them only if their reading doesn't make sense to me. I don't want to see the text because I don't want to be inadvertently influenced by the visual display. As they read, I listen for semantic and syntactic logic. I always wait for a pause in the meaning-flow to give them a chance to self-correct, and stop them only if it's clear they're not going to do so. It doesn't take long for the children to start taking over this monitoring process for themselves. Even though it requires them to put some work into the reading act, the burden is tolerable, especially since it relies heavily on one strong human attribute — the drive for meaning.

Ownership

See pages 18-19. When details and sequences get jumbled, have these children go back to check the text for confirmation.

ReQuest Procedure

This technique (Manzo, 1969) not only encourages a focus on meaning without interfering with personal style, but also fosters silent reading and higher level questioning based on that reading. Teacher and child read a short piece of text silently and then take turns asking each other questions about the content. The teacher models different kinds of questions, from literal to evaluative, and encourages good quality questions from the child.

The text is used to substantiate or disprove an answer. If the children ask me questions I can't answer I say, "Hm, I don't know that one. Show me in the text what I missed." If they misread and therefore misquestioned, or if I didn't attend carefully enough and missed something, we talk about reading more carefully. This technique takes a long time to show habitual transfer, so be patient if you choose to use it.

Self-Recording

I ask the children to record their reading and then listen, while following the text, to see if they can find places where they lost meaning. But I've learned to be careful. I use this technique only with children who have built a good level of self-confidence, who have a sense of humor and who aren't easily intimidated. Some children get upset when they hear themselves miscue, even if their miscues indicate efficient processing. Others enjoy hearing their voices recorded and respond to this exercise willingly.

Sight-Word Recognition

See pages 19-21.

I don't start sight-word work until I've spent at least a couple of weeks on supported reading and strategy-building first. Even then I limit the words to those the children choose for their own writing. Once an on-going rhythm is established for practicing these words, I start adding others from a basic list. I always monitor the practice carefully because overpredictive readers will overpredict in word practice as much as they do in their reading, and they can mislearn words if they aren't redirected on the spot. I make sure they *always* confirm a word by reading the sentences on the back of the card, not just when they aren't sure of the identification. This also helps develop the habit of self-correction.

Strategies

See pages 21-24. See also under Cloze above and concentrate on improving confirmation strategies.

Supported Reading

See pages 24-27.

I don't use taped readings with these children during recovery-work time because they usually don't attend to the print while they're listening. This doesn't mean they should be excluded from their turn at the class listening center: enjoyment of well-presented stories on tape should be a part of all children's language experience. But with the limited hours available, I don't find this an efficient use of time for recovery work. One-to-one supported reading is more effective.

Writing

See pages 27-29. Writing is "the other half" of reading and, as always, should be given equal time.

READERS MISTAKEN FOR OVERPREDICTIVE

Moving from Emergent to Early Reading

Emergent-to-early readers are in the interim stage between memory reading and using print for cues. They tend to move in and out of what would appear to be overpredictive reading behaviors. They will read a familiar text word by word when they can, but when the load becomes too tiring they will lapse back to memory reading, where they freely substitute their own interpretations.

There are two differences between children in this stage and overpredictive readers. First, their interpretations make sense: they would not be content to leave uncorrected a sentence like "Fish were seen the monster's hand," as Casey did. Secondly, they will be reading voluntarily. Overpredictive readers don't read unless they have to, because they associate reading with having impossibly difficult, meaningless tasks imposed on them. Children learning to read in an environment that allows for self-regulation *want* to read, because they are never frustrated so badly that they don't care if they ever see a book again.

Moving from Oral to Silent Reading

While developing as efficient readers, children go through a stage of fluent but poor oral reading on the way to moving fully into silent reading. As described under "Fluency" (pages 119-120), at this stage the reader's eye/brain activity is moving faster than verbalization can take place. Rather than stop and lose the semantic flow built up in his or her mind, the reader self-corrects internally. A miscue analysis can look disastrous although the retelling indicates full, detailed, well-sequenced comprehension. It's the retelling that determines the difference between overpredictive and normally developing readers.

CHAPTER 8

GLOBAL LEARNERS

EXAMPLE: MATT

Matt, Casey's brother, was 12 years old at this reading. He had earlier repeated grade one and was now just finishing his second year in grade five. A standard readiness program in his kindergarten had been followed by two years of very strictly sequenced phonemic segmentation in grade one, taught by experienced teachers. The school had then revised its language arts program with a more holistically oriented basal, one that emphasized context and sight-word building along with phonics. Daily recovery work started during Matt's second year in grade one and continued throughout his elementary years. Matt's father was above average in his non-verbal abilities but didn't read at all, despite periodic efforts throughout his adult life to learn. Matt was within the normal range in non-verbal ability.

Matt's reading of "Whiplash Escapes," from *Evaluation Resource Book for Grade Two* (Courtney, 1979) was part of the end-of-year assessment session, so he hadn't seen the material, although he was familiar with this type of session. I told him the title and subject: a pet lizard that got into trouble, and instructed him to "do the best you can" without help. The story is a mid grade two readability.

A reader fluent at this level takes between one and a half and two minutes to read this passage. Matt took 11 minutes, seven seconds. Two dots between words indicate word-by-word reading, four mean a longer pause, none shows normal fluency. I hope that seeing the complete transcript in this manner will give you the visual equivalent of what it sounded like, as well as demonstrate how Matt's "chunking" of words increased as he proceeded through the passage. I have also included a miscue-coded version of the passage to give a better idea of his overall use of strategies. (See page 124 for translation of codes used.) Note particularly his frequent corrections and use of rerun.

Misue-coded version

Whiplash is my green tree lizard. He's an interesting pet, but not everybody in our family likes him. My little brother doesn't like him because one day Whiplash ate his guppies. My mom says Whiplash is fine as long as he stays in the aquarium.

But sometimes when Mom isn't around I take Whiplash out of the aquarium. I let him run around on the kitchen table. That's what he was doing last Saturday when the phone rang. I left him for just a minute while I answered it. When I came back, Whiplash was gone. I looked all over the kitchen but I couldn't find him.

Mom came into the kitchen. "What are you looking for, Randy?" she asked.

"Oh, nothing, Mom," I said. I couldn't tell her that Whiplash was missing. Then I ran to find my sister Allison. She helped me look for Whiplash, but we couldn't find him anywhere in the house. We had to give up when Mom called the three of us for supper. I sat and looked at my plate, but I couldn't eat. Just then Allison poked me. "Look up there," she whispered. I looked up. Right on top of the grandfather's clock, I saw the tip of a green tail.

Handwritten annotations:

a; Had ©; insect in...; out; likes ©; ©P^I one day; sept gup...; Mum said; My; his; Mum © is not; fl... ©; like ©s...; telephone; © wheel ©; the phone ©Then the; with all; Robert © said; sis...ter all..; always ..also..Annie; could; anywheres.; Mum ©use; ★★3. we had gave up; 2. We had a good; 1. We went for; Can't; ★★★ Teacher re-directed; Annie spotted him; © a tail ★★★★; ...ai... ★★★★ I seen a top... tip of a green tail

★ Mmmm... mmm... What's the lizard's name?
T: You can make one up if you'd like.
Mm... I can't think of one.
T: OK. keep going.   Plootoo. One day...

© That ⓔ Mum jumped
"There's Whiplash!" I cried. Mom reached up and took him down from the clock. She put him back in the aquarium.

© Now how did you think
"Now why do you think he went up there?" she asked.
*4   he © Annie
"Maybe he thought the clock was a tree," said Allison. "After all, he is a tree lizard."

"Maybe he wanted to find out what time it was," I said.
My © thought © his
"Maybe he thinks he's a mouse," said my little brother.
                    T my Mum and me © little
My sister began to laugh, then Mom. And my brother
Jazz   © A grass   really
laughed at his own joke. I guess it was rather funny after all.

*4 Maybe he... Maybe he thought...
What's that word?
[pointing to clock]

Longhand version
T: You do the best you can.
[Pause] ... thought the clock was a tree

Text

Whiplash is my green tree lizard. He's an interesting pet, but not everybody in our family likes him. My little brother doesn't like him because one day Whiplash ate his guppies. My mom says Whiplash is fine as long as he stays in the aquarium.

Matt

Whiplash . . is . . a . . green . . tree . . lizard . . . Had . . . . He's . . an. . . . in . . . . insect . . . . pet . . but . . . . but . . . . not . . everybody . . in . . . . out family . . . Like . . him . . . My . . . . My . . . . little . . brother . . doesn't like . . him because . . I . . . . day . . . . one day . . . . Mmmmmm . . . . mmmm . . . . What's the little lizard's name? [*Teacher:* You can make one up for him if you'd like. *Matt:* Mmmm . . . I can't think of one. *Teacher:* O.K. Keep going. *Matt:* Plootoo] One day . . . . Whiplash . . ate . . his . . . . gup . . . . gept . . . . Mum . . said . . Whiplash . . is . . . . Whiplash . . is . . . . fine . . as . . long . . as . . he stays . . in his . . aquarium.

But sometimes when Mom isn't around I take Whiplash out of the aquarium. I let him run around on the kitchen table. That's what he was doing last Saturday when the phone rang. I left him for just a minute while I answered it. When I came back, Whiplash was gone. I looked all over the kitchen but I couldn't find him.

But . . sometime . . when . . Mum . . is not . . . . isn't . . around . . I take . . Whiplash . . out of . . the . . aquarium . . . I . . let him . . run . . . . around . . on . . the . . kitchen . . fl . . . . table . . . That's . . what . . he . . was . . doing . . like . . . . last . . . . S . . . . Saturday . . when the . . telephone rang . . . I . . left him . . . . left . . him . . for . . just . . a . . minute . . . . wheel . . . . while . . I . . answered the phone . . . . while I answered it . . . . while? . . . . yeah . . . . Then the . . . . When . . I . . came back . . Whiplash . . was . . gone . . . I . . looked . . all over . . the . . kitchen . . but . . I . . couldn't find him.

Mom came into the kitchen. "What are you looking for, Randy?" she asked.

Mum came into . . the kitchen . . with all . . . . "What are you . . looking for . . . . R . . Robert?" she said . . she asked.

"Oh, nothing, Mom," I said. I couldn't tell her that Whiplash was missing. Then I ran to find my sister Allison. She helped me look for Whiplash, but we couldn't find him anywhere in the house. We had to give up when Mom called the three of us for supper.

[With good expression] "Oh, nothing, Mum." I . . said . . . Couldn't . . tell her . . that Whiplash . . was . . . . was . . . . missing . . . Then I . . ran . . to find my . . sis . . sister . . . . all . . . . always . . . . also . . . . Annie . . . She . . helped . . me . . look . . for . . Whiplash . . but . . we . . could . . . . couldn't . . find . . him anywheres . . . In the house . . . We went for . . . . We . . had . . a . . good . . . . We . . had . . gave up . . when Mum called . . the three of . . the three of . . use . . . . for supper . . . . us for supper.

I sat and looked at my plate, but I couldn't eat. Just then, Allison poked me. "Look up there," she whispered. I looked up. Right on top of the grandfather's clock, I saw the tip of a green tail.

Just then . . Annie spotted him. [*Teacher:* You skipped this sentence. *Matt:* Oh!] . . . . I . . sat . . and looked . . at . . my . . plate . . but can't eat . . . Just then Annie spotted him . . . "Look up . . there" . . she . . whispered . . . I . . looked up . . . Right . . on top of . . the grandfather clock . . I saw a . . tail of . . a green . . . . t . . . . t . . ai . . l . . . . I seen a . . . . top . . . . tip . . of a greentail.

"There's Whiplash!" I cried. Mom reached up and took him down from the clock. She put him back in the aquarium.

"That . . Whiplash . . . . [good expression] There's Whiplash!" . . I cried . . . Mum jumped . . . . Mum reached up . . and . . took . . him . . down . . from the clock . . . She . . put him . . back in . . the aquarium.

"Now why do you think he went up there?" she asked.

"Now why . . did you . . . . think . . . . Now how did you . . . . think he . . went up there?" . . . . "Now why did you think he went up there?" . . she said.

"Maybe he thought the clock was a tree," said Allison. "After all, he is a tree lizard."

"Maybe he . . . . Maybe he thought . . . . [pointing to *clock*] What's that word? [*Teacher:* You do the best you can.] . . . . thought the . . clock . . was a tree," . . he . . . . said Annie . . . "After all . . he . . is . . a . . tree lizard.

Maybe he wanted to find out what time it was," I said.

"Maybe . . he . . wanted . . to . . find . . out . . what time . . it was" . . I said.

"Maybe he thinks he's a mouse," said my little brother.

"My . . . . Maybe he . . thought . . thinks . . he . . . . thinks his . . he's a mouse" . . said my little brother.

84

My sister began to laugh, then Mom. And my brother laughed at his own joke. I guess it was rather funny after all.

My sister . . . . My sister . . began to laugh. Then my mum and me . . . . And my little brother . . . . lazz . . . . And my little brother . . laughed at his . . own joke . . . A . . grass . . . . I guess . . I guess . . it was . . really funny . . after all.

Retelling

T: I want you to tell me what the story was all about.

M: It was about a lizard named Whiplash that the per . . . that got lost. He . . . when he was put on to the table to run around and get some exercise and the telephone rang and his master went to answer that and he got up on top of the clock. Him and his sister searched all over the place for it. And then they . . . the mother called them for supper and as they were eating supper his sister saw a green . . . a tip of a green tail and he said it was Whiplash's lizard . . . Ummmm . . . They put him down . . . they brought him down from there . . . from the clock and put him down . . . They brought him down from there . . . from the clock and put him back into his aquarium. And took . . . and they wondered why he was up there.

T: What reasons did they give?

M: They thought . . . well, he thought he was up there to tell time and his sister thought it might of . . . he might have thought it was a tree. And his baby brother thought he must have been a mouse . . . thought he was a mouse.

EXAMPLE: LEAH

Jane Baskwill, a Nova Scotian teacher-author, described this example to me.

Leah wanted to write the word *house* during writing workshop, using invented spelling. She listened to herself say the word "house" several times and isolated the sound associated with the initial letter. She asked herself, "What's that letter?" and then proceeded to name off the letters in her name by touching the fingers of her left hand, one by one in sequence, starting with her thumb. After naming the *h* in its sequence, she said, "Oh, it's *h*," and wrote the letter down.

EXAMPLE: PAUL

Paul and I were going through the pack of word cards put together from his last several stories, using Holdaway's procedure. He looked at the word in isolation, then checked the sentences on the back for confirmation; when he couldn't recognize the word, he used the sentences to identify it. I had also put the name of the story from which the word came in abbreviated form in one corner so we could go back to the book if we needed to. Paul went through several words, then came to one he couldn't recognize. Instead of looking at the sentences he said, "What story did that come from?"

"*The Morning Milk,*" I answered.

Replying instantly Paul said, "Oh, that's *won't*. That word is *won't*."

"How did you figure that out so quickly?"

"I just knew. When I knew the story, I knew the word."

EXAMPLE: CLARA

Clara was reading me a book she had heard several times and had been practicing on her own. She was still stumped in several places. The text said:

Who will help me?
Who will get me out of here?
I want to get out!

Clara read the first two lines steadily, word-voice matching accurately. When she got to *want* in the third line she paused, said she didn't know the word, puzzled some more, then asked me for it. I suggested she read ahead. She did, but was still puzzled. I asked her what the word started with and what sound that might represent. She told me correctly, then reread from the start and was finally able to identify the word. But then she suddenly burst out, "I know! I'll remember that word now because I always use it when I ask for a cookie. I say, 'I *want* a cookie!'" and she emphasized the strength of her feeling with a whole-body thrust as she uttered the word. The word reoccurred repeatedly throughout the story and she identified it each time by recalling her special sentence.

86

EXAMPLE: JOHN

John was one of my grade one students. He was competent at math concepts but had trouble naming numerals beyond 10. He could count easily by fives and 10's and understood the meaning of grouping numbers to count them more quickly. He also understood that two-digit numerals represent 10's and ones and he knew what that meant conceptually. But he couldn't perform operations without naming the numerals he was working with.

He was having trouble identifying the numeral 45 when I said, "All right, let's try doing this in parts. First of all let's find out what the tens column is." I put my finger under the four and said, "Count by tens until you reach this number."

He counted, and when he said "forty" he stopped and repeated, "That's forty!"

"Right! Now what's the numeral next to it?"

"Five," he answered.

"Now," I said, "put the two together: forty-five." I demonstrated by running my finger first under the four, then under the five as I said them. We practiced with a few more numerals and from then on he could name two-digit numerals using the rote memory sequence to aid the retrieval process.

DISCUSSION

Perhaps the most significant observation is that all these examples are different. Matt's transcript underscores the two common characteristics of global readers: lack of fluency and strong orientation toward meaning. But otherwise, each child has found different strategies to compensate for the lack of automaticity in the oral retrieval of word names. You can see from the examples that the children *know,* somewhere in their brains, what they are looking at. They recognize words and letters as familiar, but can't quite attach the labels. They use roundabout and unusual routes to bring up the names before the words or letters can become usable for making meaning.

PERSONAL CHARACTERISTICS

Attitude

Reading is very difficult.

Global readers who have been introduced to reading through a phonemic segmentation approach see reading as work — *hard* work. Those who have experienced a whole language approach are also frustrated, for although they see themselves making progress, they gradually become aware of how *slow* they are. Their inability to retrieve words they knew on previous occasions is demoralizing.

Reading is worthwhile.

In my experience, almost all children in this category *want* to learn to read. Each time they have a new teacher, a new approach, another tiny breakthrough, they renew their struggles. Their persistence is admirable and heartrending. It is this factor above all others that keeps me searching the literature for suggestions that might help me help their learning come more easily. The whole language approach is the beginning, but there is refining yet to be done for this small population of troubled readers.

Personality

Their intelligence is average to above.

On individual intelligence tests, global learners score within the normal range, sometimes above it, but usually with a significant gap between the verbal and performance scores, which are higher. Some younger global learners seem more evenly balanced. In any case it doesn't take I.Q. tests to determine whether a child has solid intellectual abilities: sensitive teachers and care-givers can make that assessment through careful observations.

They lack confidence.

Almost all the global learners I've known have lacked confidence in their reading ability. The older they are and the more they've been streamed, singled out, grouped and subjected to inappropriate instructional approaches, the lower their confidence level. Even those who have been in highly supportive, non-competitive environments suffer. Global learners are average to above-average in most subjects and skills — and that includes the ability to compare themselves with their peers. They know that the friends they talk and play with on an equal footing are way ahead of them in reading and, often, writing development. They are frustrated and self-conscious about the gap and easily hurt by casual deprecatory comments made by insensitive children.

They have a "right brain" orientation.

In a very broad sense, research has shown that certain areas of the brain are more responsible for some functions than others. Generally the left brain is more responsible for language functions, particularly verbalization, sequencing, ordering, logical thinking, handwriting, oral reading, etc. The right brain is used more for spatial, "global" kinds of work: art, music, dance, silent reading, possibly the creative and storage part of the writing process, building, intuition and getting a sense of the whole. The right brain seems to govern aspects of life that flow into each other, while the left governs the details, the bits and pieces.

I want to be cautious because the more we learn about the brain, the more we realize how much cross-referencing there is between the two brain hemispheres. Keeping that in mind, I find that almost every global learner I have worked with is really competent in one or more "right brain" kinds of skills or processes. Many are exceptionally good artists or builders. One became the class expert in geography and could point out on the globe — and read! — any place name that came up in discussions. He is "global" in a very literal sense! Another is an exceptional dancer who was moved into an advanced class as a result. A third had a passion for nature and extraordinary powers of observation. Noticing these things, among others, is what makes me suggest the term "global learner" for this type of troubled reader.

Reading Style

They have a strong global or holistic memory.

Global learners quickly latch onto the story-memory support system that a whole language approach provides. They seem to remember chunks of meaning quickly and accurately and rely heavily on their memory for rereading. A story they can't read at all on first viewing they often read with near accuracy after hearing only once or twice. Even when subjected to the phonemic segmentation approach, they try desperately to hold onto meaning for support. They will often respond with wonder or indignation to the weird meanings that contrived, controlled-vocabulary sentences create. It seems as though their deeper level semantic memory systems outweigh, or perhaps have developed to compensate for, their weaker surface-structure language processing systems.

These learners seem to have unusual — and holistic — systems for retrieving isolated pieces of language information:

- When trying to recall a specific isolated word, Paul only needed to hear the *title of the story* in which he had first encountered it.
- Clara discovered that she could use an emotionally loaded sentence to bring up a word. She had trouble remembering *want,* a high-frequency word but difficult because often, like many *w* words, it is neither supported by context nor phonetically consistent. After the incident described, she remembered *want* whenever she came to it by looking at the word, whispering her emphatic sentence and then restating the text sentence!
- Leah needed the support of a known sequence to recognize the identity of a letter and had established, on her own, a system for helping herself stay in sequence. Interestingly, even though she knew the letter on an intuitive level (because she knew where to find it), she couldn't *write* it just by visualizing it: she had to *hear* it first.
- John needed a similar support system for naming numerals. Like the others, he seemed to need auditory input to access recall for productive use in a linear-sequential task.

It appears to me that many of these learners don't use the

usual mechanisms for transferring bits and pieces of information from one mental storage bin to another. They don't make as many generalizations about certain kinds of information, especially language symbols, and their transferring has to be done through more global procedures. They can't access classifications automatically, the way children who learn to read quickly do.

Their eye movements are erratic.

Over the years I've noticed that many global learners have trouble keeping their eyes focused on the words they are trying to read. They skip up or down lines and frequently read several words beyond the next ones in sequence.

Reversals continue longer than usual.

Although reversals aren't exclusive to global processors, I've noticed that some of these children continue to reverse letters and words in their written work for a longer period than would be expected for normal developmental progression. However, I caution against depending on this as a consistent diagnostic marker since I've observed the same thing in the writing of good readers too.

They have an unusual visual processing style.

Perhaps because of their erratic eye movements (though I think it may be something altogether different), some global readers read words that contain the same letters as the word in the text but that are sequenced completely differently. I'm not referring simply to the traditional *was/saw* type of straight *reversal*, but to *crosshatching* of letters. Take a global processor who reads "donuts" for *buttons*. Accepting that *d* and *b* are frequently seen as the same letter, all the remaining letters match, yet note in the diagram *how* they match:

I call this "global" processing because it appears to me that these children see details in a three-dimensional way, "sprinkled" or "patterned" rather than ordered on the page in a strictly left-to-right or right-to-left sequence. Susan Sheridan, an art teacher and graduate student at the University of Massachusetts who is studying the relationship between art and writing, calls these children "pangraphic."

Their word retrieval and fluency are weak.

Until a story or passage is almost memorized, it is very difficult for global readers to read with fluency. There is a lack of automaticity between visual input and oral (or silent) and written output—again relating to the eye movement problem, perhaps, or to differences in sequential language processing.

They prefer to read orally.

My experience is that global readers resist reading silently. I have tried to encourage silent reading, hoping it would put them into another brain channel, since silent reading uses more of the right brain than oral reading does (Johnstone, 1984). But invariably they complain that it's too hard that way. They seem to need to hear themselves in order to get enough feedback for prediction and confirmation.

They tend to over-phonicate.

Global readers who have had intensive phonics drilling seem to go overboard in using these skills. It's a "tunnel thinking" similar to that shown by underpredictive readers, except that global learners try to keep meaning in mind as they read. Perhaps their problem is that they hear too many variations of sounds, especially subtle vowel variations. For example, when we teach the short *a* we assume a certain general sound to identify it. But when you listen very carefully, the *a* sound in *ham* and the *a* sound in *rat* are really quite different. Dialects account for even more pronounced variations. Most children ignore these subtle differences quite quickly, but I don't think it comes easily for global readers.

Many are left-handed males.

Among those who have had trouble long enough to need extra help, I encounter a disproportionate number of left-handed males. Among children who are slower than average breaking into reading (the six- to eight-year-old range), left-handedness and maleness are not, in my experience, common elements, although other global learning characteristics often are.

They have limited mental energy for some literary tasks.

I have found that most global learners find any linear-sequential activity mentally exhausting. They begin to show signs of fatigue (fidget, yawn, ask the time) if they are kept on a single type of sequential task for more than about 10 minutes. Reading or controlled writing exercises are more tiring than creative writing, and creative writing using a word processor seems the least exhausting.

Blakeslee (1983) observes that right brain (non-verbal) activities serve as mental recuperation: they permit the left brain to rest. Perhaps global processors, accustomed to operating though the right hemisphere, have to work so hard when they're engaging their left brain that the chemical or electrical reactions are quickly exhausted.

POSSIBLE CAUSES

There is no one single or outstanding factor that accounts for the difficulties of global learners. It's like deafness: the manifestation of the problem is the inability to hear sounds, but there is a wide variety of causes. The following section of this chapter is the product of my search through the literature that seeks to correlate physiological factors with reading difficulties. Many hypotheses are being explored, some intertwining. But people are highly complex organisms and it will take time yet to sort out causes from symptoms.

Some of the hypotheses are rather technical in nature. I've tried to translate the concepts into "normal English," however, because I think it's important to try to understand the physiology of the reading act – and abnormalities or differences that interfere with its development – so we can develop compensatory strategies and equipment. We've developed Braille and "talking books" for the blind, sign language and "phonic ears" for the deaf. If we keep working at it, we may be able to come up with equivalent aids for the global learners among us. But first we have to understand the nature of the interfering factors.

Different Brain Development

By far the greatest number of references in my reading have focused on the brain, in particular on the hemispheric differentiation that occurs. The relationship between the left and right sides (hemispheres) of the brain and the distinctive functions of the two sides are important in the reading process. There is substantial evidence that some children who are labeled "LD" (dyslexic) *do* differ physiologically from the majority of the population in the actual structures and modes of operation of their brains. Masland described some of these differences in a 1987 lecture, which I've supplemented here with additional references.

Size

The majority of human beings have a larger left side than right. As I mentioned earlier, it's the left side that is primarily responsible for certain major language activities. According to Blakeslee (1983), the left brain does most of the work for speech, handwriting, classification, object-naming, literal meanings, grammar, associating language with thought, spelling, rhythm (but not melody) and creating long, non-automatic sequences of words. (Automatic sequences would be those that are traditionally memorized as a strung-together unit such as the alphabet, days of the week, rote counting, etc.)

Some studies show that for at least some people in this class of troubled readers the reverse is true: the right side is the same size as or larger than the left. Geshwind, one of the most prominent researchers and thinkers in this field in recent times, has actually dissected several brains of deceased dyslexics and found physical proof. In discussing Geshwind's studies and brain-mapping work, Duane (1987) suggests that the cause may be a biological predisposition toward larger or symmetrical right brain formation rather than a diseased condition.

The reasons for such differences are interesting to contemplate. Perhaps a percentage of people with strong right-brain dominance was vital for our early survival as a species. Just as ants and bees produce a certain number of drones and queens to serve specialized functions, perhaps humans evolved with different brain types to serve special roles within the social structure. These people may have been the scouts and guides of the hunter/gatherer period: their ability to perceive and remember the whole environment and sense the most minute change in it would have been indispensable to a hunting party.

Electrical activity

Studies using electrical mapping of the brain show that the left hemisphere emits unusual electrical activity in some people during certain types of language-based activities.

Nerve pathways

Other studies support the conclusion that in some people the usual direct pathways from the eyes to the language-processing areas in the left hemisphere are not entirely intact, forcing the reader to use more roundabout circuits for storage and retrieval. Rosenfield (1985), in reviewing Geshwind's work, points out that there are many parts of the brain involved in the reading act. If one part isn't functioning properly, or if the fibers that carry information from, say, the visual reception area to the language processing areas are damaged, then that *route* will not serve the reading process. However, that does not mean the language areas themselves are necessarily impaired; they can be "reached" through any of several other routes: writing and tracing, sign language, perhaps art, music and dance, color imaging, evoked emotional associations, etc., some of which I will discuss among the suggestions for helping. On the other hand, Duane (1987) notes that personal histories of this type of troubled reader taken in an Isle of Wight study show an unusual prevalence of speaking disability or delay, indicating perhaps some damage to one of the language processing *areas* of the brain.

Lipa (1983) connects right hemispheric specialization in language with slow processing speed, as illustrated, perhaps, by the samples of Leah's letter-sequencing and John's number-naming:

> The left hemisphere might not be able to compete with the right hemisphere and block out conflicting information. Possibly the

student is processing words primarily with the right hemisphere, and the left hemisphere is "reciting choices" . . .

Many severely disabled readers appear to process information primarily from a holistic, cognitive view. When asked which letter of the alphabet comes before N, they must in fact say the alphabet from the beginning until they verbally arrive at the required letter. Part-whole relationships with left hemisphere processing are a definitive problem for these students. The parts are not easily separated from the whole. It is possible that the visual image is predominant and the left hemisphere must go through a step-by-step retrieval system until the "right" letter "jumps out." (p.456)

Specialization

Normally the hemispheres aren't fully specialized in their left and right functions at birth, although the propensity in 80% of infants for left-brain dominance in speech shows immediately (Restak, p.204). "Myelination," the process of sheathing nerve fibers so they can transmit impulses, takes place very gradually and nears completion by about age six (Blakeslee, p.88). If brain damage occurs before full hemispheric organization is completed, the brain is capable of reorganizing itself so that those functions normally attributed to the damaged portion are taken over by other areas. Fully mature brains can't reorganize after being damaged and recovery is much more limited (Blakeslee, pp.148-150).

While the growth process is taking place, children use both sides of their brains interchangeably, to a gradually decreasing degree as maturation and brain-side specialization occur. This might explain why younger children can so easily identify abstract shapes, including letter shapes, even when they are upside-down and backwards, and why we see more reversals in children's writing during the early years in school. Normally they outgrow this ability—or perhaps it just becomes subserved by the growing dominance of the left brain. Global processors seem to retain the ability to see abstract shapes from all angles much longer, perhaps indefinitely.

Nevertheless, many troubled readers do "outgrow" the difficulty they have in learning to read. Many catch up in fourth or fifth grade. For them it may simply be that myelination of some of the areas of the brain used for reading didn't take place between six and eight, as for most children, but during the next brain-growth spurt, between 10 and 12.

Other differences

Several additional areas of investigation are in their infancy, but promising: hormonal balance (the effect of varying levels of testosterone, the male sex hormone); immune system weaknesses (allergic and glandular influences); brain metabolism (chemical links). We need to keep an eye on the progress of this research because the potential is there for the development of some means of intervention.

Dominance of Peripheral Vision

The Associated Press (May 14/87) reported on a Gad Geiger study which indicates that some people in this category may be able to read better using their peripheral vision. Experiments with adult troubled readers who were patient and persistent have been successful. This work could explain the behavior of those children who seem to have trouble keeping their eyes focused on the words that come next in sequence, who jump above, below or far to the right.

Pavlidis (1985) found that troubled readers in this category showed eye movement patterns and characteristics different from those of other readers.

Genetic Propensity

It has long been suspected that trouble learning to read may be an inherited trait. Perhaps the rapidly developing technology for studying genes may soon provide some physical proof. Shelley Smith may have found such evidence already. In a speech at the 1987 annual Orton Society Conference, she presented evidence correlating chromosomal links with learning-to-read difficulties. Using a variety of statistical analyses, she and her team were able to identify one or more genes linked to reading difficulties among selected families in which there had been significant numbers of troubled readers for three generations. Not all such families show evidence of genetic linkage, however.

It may just be that in very well defined dyslexics, they have a common problem no matter what their etiology [cause] is until we know how to look at things that are very very basic to the reading process. For example Dr. [Bruce] Pennington has looked at the spelling errors that are in these families and Dr. Richard Olson . . . has looked at twin studies in trying to determine what types of spelling errors . . . show the most genetic influence. What both Dr. Pennington and Dr. Olson found was that areas involving phonemic coding seemed to be the ones that are seen in this dyslexic population no matter what their linkage status [probability for heritability] is and is shown up as being the most heritable in the twin studies. So it may be that we haven't got to the point of breaking down the reading process enough or we're not looking at the right aspects to be able to tell these [genetic from non-genetic links] apart.

She went on to explain that a heritable gene connected with reading ability or difficulty may only affect "certain points in this complicated pathway of reading," and that is the hypothesis under which her team is currently working.

I find this conclusion encouraging because it implies that only part of the system is disrupted. If we can find the routes that are intact, that operate well, we can help these children learn to read. That's the hypothesis under which *I* work.

Inappropriate Instruction

If global readers are limited to a single strategy for making meaning from print, they are doomed from the start. They need to make use of every means possible, with the heaviest reliance on whatever mode of operation turns out to be *their* personal strength. Too often remediation simply intensifies decoding and rule-learning and de-emphasizes (even forbids!) the use of context, sight-word building, integrational strategies, emotional associations and personally developed compensatory strategies. If adding rule-based instruction truly helps an individual become a more efficient reader, it should be included as part of the remedial work. But if the child is spending more time recalling which rules to apply to a single word than in working for the meaning of the whole, such instruction is reducing rather than enhancing efficiency.

Lack of Confidence

Lack of confidence begins as a symptom rather than a cause. However, once a poor self-image becomes a state of being, it aggravates and magnifies the problem for these children by causing them to avoid independent reading and to give up on themselves as potential readers.

Male Predominance

In her summary of genetic linkages Smith (1987) suggests that the predominance of males in this category may not be as large or definitive as we have believed. Although her team did find more boys with reading trouble, the families they studied had more boys in them to begin with. They also found that the difficulties of affected girls weren't usually as severe. Severe cases in the girls tended to improve with age, although for the boys they didn't. Her present conclusion is that the ratio is closer to 50/50, but that the manifestation of reading difficulties drops among females as they grow, for reasons yet undetermined. However, the children she is working with are selected specifically for their potential to test genetic linkage, which excludes those whose difficulties come from other causes. The fact is, we still see more boys in special help groups.

There are a number of theories put forth to explain that. Duane (1987) describes Geshwind's hypothesis that testosterone levels may have something to do with left-brain development and this possibility is being investigated. It is generally accepted that boys develop more slowly than girls, and Blakeslee notes that early maturers are statistically better at verbal tasks, late maturers at spatial tasks:

> The one mental difference between men and women that experts can agree upon is that women are generally superior at verbal tasks and men are superior at spatial ability. It appears that this is a biological difference caused by the faster maturation and reduced lateralization of the female (p.103).

"Lateralization" means independence of operation by the two hemispheres — "taking sides," if you will.

The slower maturational process in males allows each hemisphere to specialize its own functions more thoroughly before the nerve fibres joining the two have become operational. Boys have more time to build a strong, well-organized visual-spatial right hemisphere and to attend and organize speech sounds in the left. My conclusion would be that since the left hemisphere dominates in language, the faster-maturing girls are locked into that domination because they have less time to organize the right hemisphere. Their visual-spatial abilities end up operating from both hemispheres. It should be noted that slow-maturing girls follow the same developmental pattern as boys and end up with stronger spatial abilities. The problem in reading can come when, for some reason, a child doesn't develop proper lateralization. Damage during development can throw off the process, and since boys develop more slowly, the opportunities for damage to occur are greater.

Cultural expectations are also often cited as the reason for male predominance. Kenneth Goodman (1976) offers his explanation in this vein:

> It is very interesting that if you walk into any remedial reading classroom . . . you can predict that the large majority of the kids in the remedial reading program are going to be males compared to females. Unless somebody can demonstrate, and I don't believe they can, that there is some kind of sex-linked gene that keeps people from learning to read, I think we have to accept that simply as another evidence that boys, for cultural reasons, are often less willing to conform than girls are to the kinds of demands we make on them and the limits we set on what we accept and what we won't. (p.21)

I could counter by suggesting that perhaps girls are more adaptable and have a better ability to overcome the obstacles that are often set in the path of literacy acquisition. Neither explanation helps these troubled boys, however, and such arguments serve only to distract us from an investigation of causes. The evidence of differences stands on its own. The proper point to be made, and Goodman does make it, is that we have to readjust our demands and acceptable limits to meet the needs of all differences, regardless of their nature or origin.

The educational implications are as serious for girls as for boys. Perhaps the reason I am still unable to do an Eskimo roll in a kayak after five years of trying, while both my husband and son were able to do one on the first try, is that I didn't have enough spatial and motor experiences in early childhood, when my right hemisphere needed extra stimulation to compensate for the dominating influence of the left! As we value right-brain abilities more and more, girls may be the ones filling future remedial classes. Our real task is to learn as much as we can about *differences* — not insist that they don't exist or that they aren't important — so we can develop educational procedures that accommodate them.

Neurological Diseases or Traumas

I have worked with three global learners who make me wonder if certain neurological diseases or traumas don't have an influence on reading troubles. One child has mild cerebral palsy, one suffers from muscular dystrophy, and the mother of the third suffers from multiple sclerosis, a degenerative disease of the myelin sheathing that surrounds nerve fibers. All three children are males, but none is left-handed and none has a father with reading problems. In fact, the fathers of two are college graduates.

Cerebral palsy is caused by brain damage. Muscular dystrophy is hereditary and progressive and results in the wasting away of muscle tissue. With multiple sclerosis, there may be a genetic tendency toward abnormal myelin development. "Myelination" (Itzkoff, 1985) has been cited as a possible cause of reading difficulties since, without the sheath of fatty insulation called "myelin," nerves can't transmit impulses. If there is a delay in the development of the sheathing around certain nerves in the brain, and those nerves happen to be the ones responsible for the kind of thinking involved in the reading process, learning to read would logically be more difficult.

Rigid Time-Frame Expectations

I worked with a brother and sister who were both within the average range of intelligence and whose father had also had trouble learning to read. Both children were reading on grade level by the time they reached grade five, in spite of being two years or more behind during most of their reading career before that time. Their difficulty learning to read may have been caused by delayed specialization of the left hemisphere. When another brain growth spurt began between 10 and 12, the reading process came together for them.

Such children begin early to think of themselves as failures. The problem is that educators and parents still hold the traditional expectation that children *should* learn to read between six and eight. Our curricular planning is tied into that expectation, as are our materials. Our instructional format doesn't accommodate non-literate learning beyond grades one or two. We don't assume that a blind person can succeed in a regular school environment. Why can't we accept that global readers *will* learn to read, though a little later, perhaps, than average students? Allowing them to master the basic curriculum through alternative means (while, of course, continuing to help them a great deal with their reading!) would take pressure off both them and ourselves.

Unusual Auditory Acuity

Sometimes I wonder if there may be a connection between auditory distractibility and the need to read orally. I find I must read aloud if I am to grasp a difficult piece of text while reading in a noisy room. Perhaps global readers have highly attuned auditory systems that make them susceptible to the slightest external distraction. To drown out the distracting noise, they must make their own. Williams (1983, p.24) points out that the right hemisphere relies only on general acoustic clues and so has trouble sorting speech from background noise. Reading aloud may force employment of the left-brain to help with the speech-vs-noise sorting process.

FOCUS FOR RECOVERY

Reminder: In my discussion of universal principles (Chapter 3) I included a number of points I consider *vital* for any recovery program. Those points are not repeated here, but please don't forget them! Other important concepts are described in the glossary.

Confidence

See pages 16-17. This one is *vital!*

Enjoyment

See pages 17-18.

All the researchers agree on this point: global learners need practice. It's often phrased as "overlearning," but that term can imply boredom and drudgery and refer solely to skills drilling. I prefer to talk about "practice," and when I discuss it with my children I make an analogy with learning to walk or ride a bike or swim — when you want to learn something, you practice a lot. That makes sense to them.

Practice is important for all readers, but global readers need special attention. "Natural" readers — those who learn without formal coaching — practice all the time on their own. Because they find reading difficult, global readers often avoid practicing. They need some extra time just to read with the teacher or with willing parents, an older student, a volunteer, a resource person. Reading *can* be enjoyable to them if it's done through supported-reading techniques, and if the materials are student-chosen.

Experience of Fluency

Global readers' lack of fluency, unlike that of underpredictive readers, isn't necessarily due to poor prediction strategies. In fact, one of the characteristics of global readers is that they strive for meaning. When encouraged to use every available strategy, they *do* make meaning from text. Matt's reading of "Whiplash Escapes" is a prime example of this. In spite of the slow pace of his reading he made only three substitutions that caused a meaning loss: "insect" for *interesting*, "out" for *our*, and "gept" for *guppies*. All three were in the first paragraph before he had built up a story-base on which to predict. After that, everything he read made sense in its corrected form, and his retelling clearly shows how well he held the story in mind. Even before correction, his miscues showed meaning orientation: he started to say "floor" when he read "I let him run around on the kitchen fl . . . table" and later, when they found the lizard, he read "'There's

Whiplash,' I cried. Mum jumped . . . Mum reached up . . ." Both show logical prediction. Given these indications at the word level, and his excellent comprehension of the story, it's hard to understand how it could take him six times longer than average to read it!

We can give these children some help for developing fluency. Supported-reading techniques usually help, but global readers don't seem to transfer the fluency they gain in a known situation to a new text, even when all the vocabulary and the general topic are the same. What supported reading does do is provide the *experience* of fluency so the children know what to strive for.

The use of peripheral vision may be another key. I've developed a technique I call "finger leading," which makes use of the child's peripheral vision. I choose a text that is already partially familiar, then sit opposite the child so that I'm reading upside down. Keeping a steady pace slightly faster than the child reads independently, I move my finger just above the words and instruct the child to try to keep up with it. I find I can use this technique only for very short periods, however; it seems to be quite tiring.

Left-to-Right Sequencing

Reading material at their independent level will have the added advantage of providing practice for left-to-right visual sequencing. It is more efficient to remediate this difficulty while reading than to take separate time for visual tracking exercises that aren't related to the reading act.

Oral/Aural Reading

If global readers need to read aloud to slow up and control their active peripheral vision, then encouraging the use of that strength may eventually resolve the need—although that connection has yet to be proven. If, on the other hand, these readers have to *hear* in order to *understand,* because auditory processing is an integral part of their circuitry, then they may always have to read aloud, or at least subvocalize. They may need to listen to texts before trying to read them independently for years longer than the average learner does. If a third alternative is true—that the hearing of global learners is so sensitive that they are distracted by minor sounds around them to such a degree that they can't concentrate—then the use of headphones to block out noise might be a helpful solution in moving them toward silent reading. All of these possibilities need further investigation at the classroom level.

Peripheral Vision

The use of peripheral vision is a new discovery and yet to be fully proven, but it may be worth trying with children who show erratic or unusual eye functioning. The technique used in the study was to have a dot on a sheet of paper and a hole starting 3.5 cm (1.4") to the right of the dot and large enough to allow viewing of eight or nine letters. The reader moved the sheet across the line of print, looking at the dot while reading the words. The researchers emphasized that the technique works only with highly motivated, patient people. (AP article, 5/12/87).

Phonetic Analysis

Blending is useless, especially for global learners, in spite of the fact that it seems to be used almost universally as the core of recovery programs. Vellutino (1986) distinguishes between "synthetic phonics" and a more whole-word kind of analysis. By his definition, synthetic phonics is "where students are taught each letter-sound association in isolation"—not the system he used in his research. His instruction was "designed to teach children to detect and abstract letter-sound associations in printed 'words' presented as wholes." It's my interpretation that he was working more with the word family concept that I use than with the traditional blending process. It reminds me of the old Merrill linguistics program, which I've used successfully for short periods by adding to it and reinforcing it with the other strategies. I think this is the way to approach phonetic analysis —and I *do* think global readers need practice with these skills *once they have meaning-getting strategies well in place.* They need every skill and strategy they can get, provided everything is always focused around meaning.

Rerouting

Instead of always redirecting global learners to the details of print for decoding, I think we need to capitalize on the natural tendencies they already possess. Since the usual system of building associations among words by their visual and phonic similarities is very difficult for them, we need to make use of the "routes" the children themselves have discovered for remembering and associating. The reading samples of Leah, Clara, John and Paul reveal the personal systems they have developed for naming words and letters they recognize non-verbally.

Leah used her name as a place where she knew she could name the letter *h*. Her name was perhaps the most emotionally powerful word she knew; if they know no other words, children know their names and, usually, how to spell them. Leah used her fingers to maintain sequence and oral naming to identify the letter. She developed the strategy herself, but I could have taken advantage of it by helping her build a small bank of "key words"—especially potent words that Leah chose to learn herself—and encouraging her to use them when she couldn't remember a particular letter in isolation.

Clara thought of a high-impact phrase from a meaningful situation to help her remember a particularly difficult sight word. Using the same principle, she worked with her father to build a sight-word bank. She chose personally meaningful words, copied them in standard spelling, wrote a sentence or short story based around each, and illustrated her efforts. This is a technique Sylvia Ashton-Warner documented (1963). Not only did Clara never forget those words, but she began to use them for making associations with other words she encountered.

Paul's routing was the most global of any child I've worked with. He seemed to store individual words in mental "story boxes"—needing only the title to trigger the identity of any word within it. Once I discovered that, I used titles as the cues on his word cards for his reading of new stories and in association-building.

If it's true that these learners are right-brain dominant, either because the left side has a defect or because it's simply natural to them to be "right-brained" in the same way it's natural to have a hand preference, it seems logical that we should allow them to make maximum use of that preference. If we observe them closely as they read and write (without interruption), sooner or later we will see that they've discovered a personal key.

The problem with programs that stress drilling in phonics and word-attack rules is that they tend not to encourage the development of the personal strengths of the learners. Some approaches discourage the use of meaning-getting strategies and self-correction. Both the teacher and other students stop and correct the readers before they've had a chance to discover their own mistakes. If we forbid them the use of their personal strategies for gaining meaning, they will, quite literally, never do any real reading during their school years.

Rotation of Activities

I keep sessions on highly focused details short and relevant to reading. I intersperse reading with writing and doing the purposeful activities the reading prepared for in the first place. For example, we:
- read or reread for 10 minutes;
- practice 10 words using word cards (or a computerized Holdaway list) for five to 10 minutes;
- spend 10 minutes writing, using invented spelling (preferably on a word processor);
- finish with working on illustrations for a story that has already been typed.

Sight-Word Recognition

See pages 19-21.

I especially recommend developing a computerized version of Holdaway's list, or any other list of basic sight words, for these children. It doesn't require complicated programing and is especially motivating for the learners. (You might write to Steve Baskwill, R.R.#1, Lawrencetown, Nova Scotia, Canada BOS 1MO for details.) Just make sure any program you use provides the option to call up the sentences for word identification *in context*. It's my experience that working through the list once isn't enough. Matt, for example, after working through the list for a year, forgot about half the words over the summer and needed to work through it again the second year. He was also working on words on cards from his reading and writing.

Simultaneous Instruction

I stick this in to catch your attention and once again slip in mention of the importance of carrying out as much recovery work as possible *during the process of real reading and writing.* Most of the suggestions here take no more than 15 to 30 seconds of "instruction," interspersed as needed during a reading session. Such spontaneous instruction includes:

Silence

Deliberate silence is one of the most powerful one-to-one instructional tools I use. It promotes:
- thinking *(Looks like I'm going to have to figure this out for myself.);*
- self-correction *(Looks like she's going to give me the time I need to make it make sense.);*
- independence *(Looks like I'm on my own—she's not taking it over for me.);*
- confidence *(Hey, man, I did it all by myself!).*

Context comments

Use of context is built through comments like: "What can you do now?" or "Try reading ahead for more clues."

Self-correction comments

Self-correction is built through: "Did that make sense?" or "Try that one again, I'm not sure I understood it."

Risk-taking comments

Risk-taking is encouraged with: "Try it and see if it works" or "Keep going" or "What do *you* think?" or "You see? It worked!"

Graphophonic comments

Associations between known and new in terms of graphophonics can be supported with comments like: "That word rhymes with _____" or "That's in the same family as _____" (quickly jot down the associated word) or "That's like the word you figured out earlier when ___"

Strategies

See pages 21-24.

Since meaning-making is such a strength for global processors, they should be encouraged to use meaning-getting strategies to their fullest. Sense-making strategies will often compensate for reversals, and prediction strategies will help compensate for over-phonication. These children also need lots of *time* to self-correct. Don't interrupt!

Supported Reading

See pages 24-27.

Don't ignore this one! Supported reading is especially necessary for global learners; in fact, they may need it for years longer than average learners. One private reading clinic uses, as the core of its recovery program, taped readings customized to the individual learner's reading style and the type of material (Carbo, 1984). My own preference is to work one-on-one, interacting with the content and discussing word meanings, unusual constructions, word features, opportunities for using certain strategies, etc. as we go along.

Visual/Phonic Associations

Since global learners seem to have difficulty making instantaneous visual and phonic (surface structure) associations, we should make use of their strong meaning and emotion-based systems to help them build these associations. (Emotional involvement comes from the right hemisphere!) I constantly refer children to other situations where they encountered words that momentarily stumped them. "That's a word you figured out in ___" or "That's in the title of the story about ___" or "You read that word in the last sentence. Can you find it?"

Clara gave us an example of an emotion-based association. Another child, from a close-knit family, had great difficulty identifying the word *other*, yet he knew *mother* as an automatic sight word because of its emotional impact. He learned the word when I wrote *mother,* then helped him separate the /m/ sound from it to get *other.* Each time he encountered *other* we went through this process until, little by little, I was able to reduce my part in the procedure: I would write *mother* and simply cover the *m*, letting him verbalize the association alone; next I would write only *mother;* then, the letter *m;* then I would just grab the paper and get ready to write. Finally, whenever he came to *other* he would look up at me with a twinkle and let the mental wheels turn silently as he came up with the identification himself.

Word Patterns

Once global readers have grasped the basic strategies and processes of reading (left-to-right/top-to-bottom flow, word-voice matching, use of context, etc.), have read books through supported reading techniques for at least a year, and have developed a basic bank of sight words, regular study of word patterns becomes useful. I use "word patterns" rather than "phonics." Phonics implies blending instruction, which is not usually helpful to these children because of the closely sequenced nature of the activity. It's more helpful to identify familiar chunks in a word than to sound it out from left to right.

In addition to the ideas already described above for building sight-word recognition, I include lists of word families as the equivalent of word cards in the packet of sight words we review each session, always making sure the first word is one the child knows by sight. When the entire list can be read through quickly, the words can be put on separate cards and mixed in with the general collection. In the meantime, when the child is reading and has trouble with a word that belongs to the word family under study I say something like: "That word is from one of your word families." Or I might quickly write down a known word from the family with the problem word right under it. It's important to keep referring all isolated work back to real reading situations.

Writing

Last, and most important, is writing practice. See pages 27-29.

I'm convinced that writing, using invented spelling, is going to be the key to unlocking reading for many global learners. Among readers who make average progress I regularly see significant breakthroughs in reading right after new awarenesses shows up in their writing. The corresponding breakthroughs are even more dramatic with some global learners who have been doing a lot of writing.

I had a global learner in my grade one class not long ago who had repeated kindergarten in his previous school and was in need of some morale building. Although he had a strong meaning orientation, his reading progress in terms of what he could handle independently was painfully slow, and he was exceptionally sensitive about the "good" reading he observed among the other children. About midway through the year he discovered that writing was an outlet and began writing avidly both at home and at school. Within two or three weeks of his personal commitment to writing I began to see him making new connections in reading, and during the last six weeks of school he was making rapid progress in both the acquisition of sight words and the ability to use graphophonic cues. This rate of progress continued the following year in a grade two whole language classroom, and by the end of that year he was reading on grade level.

I believe the connection may, again, have to do with right and left brain usage. The television series *The Brain* showed experiments with split-brain patients, people in whom the two halves of the brain had been surgically separated for medical reasons. One woman was shown a picture of someone performing a particular activity, but she could look at it only with her left eye—which required the use of the right hemisphere, the spatially oriented, non-verbal side of the brain. When asked to name the activity, she couldn't. When asked to *write* the name of the activity, using her left hand, her written word was correct, yet she still couldn't name it orally. It wasn't until she was shown the word with her right eye that she knew what the left side had seen. This shows that the right hemisphere does possess language and the ability to label, though not through the voice box.

My speculation is that if global learners have a tendency to be right-brain dominant or hemispherically unspecialized, and if they have trouble making connections through the verbal storage and retrieval system, then using the right brain's capacity to label through writing would be a logical means of approaching literacy. They would be learning the same connections between the written symbol system of language and meaning, but would be short-cutting the verbal storage and retrieval system. The oral connection would be developed through reading back their own writing. It's the old language experience approach except that the original drafts are written by the child, not dictated to the teacher.

Another way to draw on right brain strength may be to encourage typing (with both hands!) on the word processor. I'm quite certain that I use more of my brain when I type than when I write by hand. One indication is that what I write often surprises me, especially when I read it aloud. I know more and can express myself more fully than I thought. I think I'm actually pulling in more information by adding my left hand to the job! I also make many more reversals and "right-brain" kinds of errors when I type. This sort of hypothesizing may seem far-fetched and unprofessionally speculative, but I think it's worth investigating. Perhaps one way to test the idea would be to do PET scans of people writing both ways.

Invented spelling

Allowing writing to be done in invented spelling removes the burden from children of having to remember standard spellings. It also focuses attention on letter-sound correspondences, which often need extra practice anyway. I had one child whose mother understood the concept of invented spelling well and gave her son words to practice orally as part of their bedtime together-time. She knew how to keep it fun and well paced. Shortly after she started, the boy had a major breakthrough in both reading and writing at school.

Language experience stories

Since global learners have such a strong meaning orientation, using their own stories as reading material works well. I encourage my children to do as much of the writing of these stories as they can, then take dictation for the rest. Sometimes I alternate with them. Then I type the stories, leave spaces for illustrations, and bind the pages into books. The finished products can be used for focusing on details and skills, like any other material.

Word processing

Writing involves at least three sequencing activities: story sequence, drawing sequence (formation of letters) and phonic sequence. Once a child has achieved some familiarity with the keyboard, a word processor removes the drawing sequence from the process. There are two other benefits: writing on a word processor is motivating (perhaps it draws on enjoyment associated with watching television or playing arcade games) and it helps with spelling. I find that children recognize when a word doesn't "look right" more easily when it's in standard typeface than when it's written by hand. It makes sense: typeface is the way we usually see words; handwriting is a different alphabet, visually speaking. Since spelling difficulty is often a global characteristic, this is an important factor.

ADDITIONAL NOTES

I have read or heard estimates that as many as 20% of children are "learning disabled"—children who would qualify for specially funded resources or programs. But two to four percent is my estimate of truly disabled children—children with a processing style so different that learning to read is a slow, difficult task no matter how it's approached. As a resource teacher in a rural Canadian school of about 380 students, I seldom worked with more than seven or eight children in a given year that I would identify as global processors. The remainder of my troubled reader workload could be accounted for by the other categories, by physical, emotional or maturational factors, or by inappropriate instruction or expectations. And my experience is in line with studies cited by Masland (1987) on the Isle of Wight, which found that about four percent of the population had severe difficulty learning to read.

There is a call for early diagnosis of the children I label global learners. But with the diagnostic tools we use now, the danger is that we will label children too soon and place them in programs that may be just the opposite of what they really need.

I think *many* very young children are global learners because the hemispheric specialization is still taking place, and I'm not convinced we can determine clearly before age nine or 10 whether a child is going to be one of those who will always have trouble with literacy activities. Even that is too early if the child is one of those whose nerve development isn't completed until the pre-puberty brain-growth spurt.

We need to know more. We need definitive correlations between specific learning styles and physiological characteristics that show up at birth, such as brain size or electrical emission differences. For example — and this is strictly hypothetical — we might find through longterm studies that children who are right-brain dominant at birth and who show a particular electrical emission pattern from a certain part of the brain may consistently learn to read best through touch. Perhaps Braille could be their route to literacy.

Such speculations may sound untenable at this point. But then, not many people imagined walking on the moon a few generations back either. I believe we have the means to solve this problem. All we need is the will.

GLOSSARY OF
TERMS

Every field of study, every movement, every sub-group develops its own jargon because, psychologists tell us, jargon gives the group members a sense of belonging and exclusivity, of "being in." When we're working to include people in a new way of thinking, the effort to be exclusive is hardly helpful. In the case of the whole language movement, Ken Goodman calls this attitude being "wholier than thou"(Goodman, 1986). But I think it's more than that, and it doesn't have to have negative connotations or functions. Jargon can facilitate communication by allowing people who work in the same field to converse more accurately and efficiently. Unfortunately, the words sometimes degenerate into generalizations or misrepresentations of the original concepts and need to be redefined or replaced.

Whole language people have grown a healthy crop of jargon — terms that sprout and flourish whenever like minds come together. Many are coined or adapted from elsewhere, and some are obscure or complex enough that a book like this can't provide the necessary fullness of meaning for readers who are new to the whole language philosophy of literacy learning. Some are already becoming abused. Many have taken on personally colored meanings as individual experience has grown.

I include this glossary to clarify what *I* mean by some of the words and phrases I use *within the context of this book*. Those of you who are already acquainted with whole language will be able to compare your own understandings with mine and accommodate the differences you find. For those new to the philosophy, this section can serve as an initial reference and help you become familiar with some of the "language of whole language."

BLEND

A blend is a cluster of two or more consonants in which the common sound of each consonant is discernible, although it's often difficult to decode the letters separately without losing the blended sound they represent. Some of the common blends taught in basal reading programs are:

- *r* blends *(br, cr, dr, fr, gr, pr* and *tr)*
- *l* blends *(bl, cl, fl, gl, pl* and *sl)*
- *st* and *str* blends.

Others include such combinations as *sc, sk, sw, sm, sp,* etc.

CLOZE

Cloze is a fancy term for "closure." It refers to a variety of techniques in which words are left out of a text so that readers can replace them using context only or, sometimes, limited graphophonic cues. My choice of "gaps" depends on the particular strategy I want to emphasize at the time. For more detail see page 22; see also Oral Cloze below.

CONFIRMATION STRATEGIES

See Prediction and Confirmation Strategies.

CUEING SYSTEMS

As defined by miscue research, three of the language systems on which we rely for cues as we seek meaning from text are:

- semantic (based on meaning)
- syntactic (based on grammar)
- graphophonic (based on surface display and letter-sounds)

Everything people do they do within a context and with expectations of some sort, including reading. If we are handed a book to read, our knowledge of the personality of the giver will carry expectations for the content. My friend who loves science fiction hands me a book called *Dune* and I anticipate a story about a dry, desert world. My friend from Cape Cod hands me the same book and I anticipate a piece of poetic prose on the beauties of the shore. Even reading a list of words is done within a context: a shopping list signals food words or needed items that have been discussed or anticipated previously; a guest list tells me to anticipate people's names; a word list in a testing situation tells me I am restricted to one cueing system — my knowledge of graphophonics, especially my bank of sight words.

Whole texts (including the single- or limited-word texts found on signs and cereal boxes) are supported by all three sets of cues. We expect a certain kind of meaning, particular grammatical structures and a graphic display that includes letters, though not necessarily being limited to them. We see road signs and *semantically* we anticipate commands, instructions, information and repetition; *syntactically* we anticipate only key words and a limited, consistent vocabulary used over and over; *graphically* we anticipate large, clear lettering, color and shape coding, and a multitude of symbols that carry universal meanings, such as arrows, green circles, red bisected circles, telephone receivers, etc. It's the predictability of the total context that allows us to read the words almost instantly, often before we can make out the individual letters.

For more complete definitions of each system, check below under the individual headings. For a more in-depth discussion of this topic refer to *Findings of Research in Miscue Analysis: Classroom Implications* (Allen and Watson, 1976).

DIGRAPH

"Digraph" can have two meanings. It can refer to two consecutive letters representing a single sound that no letter alone normally represents: *sh, ch, th, wh, ph* and *ng,* or it can refer to two consecutive letters that represent any single sound, such as the vowel digraph *ea* in *head* or *bead.*

EARLY READER STAGE

I use "early reader" to describe the stage of reading beyond "emergent." This stage, when children are working on adding print cues to their collection of reading strategies, is characterized by a severe slowdown in oral reading. The children have become aware that print carries much of the message and their reading style has changed:

• They word-voice match as they read.
• They use their store of sight words to provide context.

- They use initial consonant letter-sound correspondences as memory-triggers.
- They try to connect print cues to picture cues and story memory.

I think this is the most sensitive and potentially difficult stage, a time when it's important to let children find their own way and set their own pace. It's a complex time in reading development because the readers are suddenly faced with the knowledge that they must gain an understanding of that overwhelming mass of symbols spread out on the page if they are really to "get at" the process called reading. They should be allowed to continue to use reconstruction of text whenever they get "bogged down" in the print; generally they exhibit much shifting back and forth between memory-based story reconstruction and direct use of print, depending on the level of their print knowledge or its applicability in a given context.

I always have two or three children each year who, when they make the early reader breakthrough, enthusiastically, persistently and demandingly take on print mastery as the major challenge in their lives. They seem tireless in their drive to incorporate the graphophonic system into their repertoire of skills and strategies. But for others this stage can be exhausting, especially if there is too much pressure to rely heavily on print before they are ready. My own son completely rejected personal involvement with books for a while during this stage. He was in a pure phonics program, totally sequential and cumulative, with an absence of meaningful context. Children who are overwhelmed by the discovery of print need gentle, sensitive coaching and encouragement. Pressure or anxiety from those around them will tend to block commitment to the process of mastering print.

EFFICIENT READING

By "efficient reading" I mean the use of a minimum of time and effort to gain meaning from a text. Time is not spent correcting a miscue that didn't cause meaning loss. Time is not spent sounding out an unnecessary word or a word more easily identified through context. Fluency is as good as the reader's developmental stage and personal style permit.

In my experience, the children who are on the road to efficiency are those whose eyes and minds seem to be everywhere at once. Their eyes dance over the page, from the target word or phrase-chunk to pictures, to previously read words, back to target words, on to the coming words. Sometimes their glance will take them around the room in search of a suspected clue on a familiar chart or sign. They constantly apply logic and their sense of language to the task. They use everything they can get their eyes and brains on to help them proceed through their text. Above all, they are focused on holding together the meaning. They are quick to pick up meaning loss or discrepancies between their predictions and what they've read. They are critical readers who judge texts stringently, question and try to explain to themselves why something might have been written in an unusual way. Efficient readers are flexible readers who adapt their reading style and strategies to the kind of text before them and the circumstance in which they find themselves.

EMERGENT READER STAGE

This stage extends from birth to the early reader stage. Emergent readers read essentially without using print. They understand that a text contains a particular meaning and they reconstruct that meaning by using their understanding and memory of the ideas, context, purpose and, if the text is a book, the pictures and such cues as page-turning. The more familiar they are with a text, the closer their reconstruction will come to the author's text. Word-voice matching and other indications of an awareness of print are not used at this stage, except perhaps for signs in pictures or visually emphasized words. Reading is more of a "retelling" that conforms in overall meaning and correspondence to the original but that relies on the reader's interpretation and choice of vocabulary, timing and sense of page-matching.

FLUENCY

Fluency acts as a carrier of language flow and a binder of meaning. However, it's important to understand that there are different stages of fluency for children who are learning to read.

Emergent readers are highly fluent because they are essentially reading from within their own language structures and understanding of the text. That is, they are practicing "reading-like behavior" by reconstructing text while using pictures, page-turning sequences and other non-print cues to regulate their passage through the story or poem. This is an important stage in the process: it allows children to experience the fluency they see mature readers using, an experience they will strive to regain when subsequent stages slow them down.

When children discover that print is the primary vehicle for the message, their fluency slows down drastically for a while as they learn the skills and strategies for using that print for cue-taking. As they become more efficient in using print, fluency picks up again.

The next decline in oral reading quality occurs when readers enter the silent reading stage. At this point the eye and brain move faster than the mouth and many uncorrected miscues show up in analysis, although comprehension remains high.

Finally, fully mature readers adjust their fluency to the types of material and the purposes for reading. Fluency is also a matter of individual style. Some readers with very accurate comprehension read very slowly, but careful scrutiny shows a steadiness of flow that is not present in the reading of someone with both poor fluency and poor comprehension. Individual styles aside, generally the goal is to work for an even, comfortable flow.

FRUSTRATION LEVEL

See Reading Levels.

GRAPHOPHONIC CUEING SYSTEM

One of the sets of cues we use to get an author's message is the arrangement of letters-into-words on the page. The visual symbols (letters) make up the "graphic" display. The "phonic" part of the system is the sound that the various combinations of letters represent when we use them orally in a particular context. (Remember, homonyms need context to determine sound representation.)

Efficient readers use the graphophonic system to sample the text for cues in order to keep the predictions they make in line with the author's intended message. They do not closely examine a word unless they experience meaning loss, but rather use a variety of possible hints, such as word length, word shape or outstanding features like double letters, initial letter-sound correspondences, or common endings (-*ing*, -*tion*, -*s*, -*ed*, etc.). Any one or any combination of hints may be sufficient to confirm a prediction.

If the meaning continues to flow as anticipated, closer scrutiny isn't necessary. However, if the message suddenly doesn't make sense, readers go back and take a closer look at the details of the word, focusing on one of its features to establish identification. They may apply skills such as blending the letter-sounds, looking for the word's relationship to other known words (for example, *other* is in the same pattern as *mother*), or breaking the word into syllables. Throughout this very rapid study they keep the sentence and passage context in mind, and at the instant they hit upon a logical word for that context the study is abandoned and reading is continued.

Use of phonics skills is a last resort for the efficient reader: expectations for meaning based on background knowledge, previous text, purpose for reading, awareness of the grammatical logic of language (developed throughout the preschool years) and contextual clues supported by automatically recognized sight words are all used in the reading process *before* phonic and specific word-recognition skills are brought into service.

For more details, refer to Menosky's discussion in *Findings of Research in Miscue Analysis* (Allen and Watson, pp. 75-79).

INDEPENDENT LEVEL

See Reading Levels.

INSTRUCTIONAL LEVEL

See Reading Levels.

INVENTED SPELLING

Invented spelling is simply a tool for children to use until they know how to use standard spelling. When writing a rough draft for the purposes of recording ideas or information, or when writing for personal pleasure, children spell words the way they think they look and sound. Invented spellings should be accepted totally and unequivocally by others since the purpose is to capture ideas before they get away. If the writing is to be put on public display at a later time, or read by people other than the writer, it may have to be translated into standard spelling with the help of someone who knows the standard.

LINEAR-SEQUENTIAL

This refers to the left-to-right, top-to-bottom nature of the graphic display of written language. Although we don't read strictly left to right (efficient readers allow their eyes to do considerable roaming around for additional cues within, before and beyond the target word they are identifying), basically the brain has to cope with a set of symbols that are displayed in a line and in a sequence. The eye-brain coordination must be able to perform a steady forward/return movement while processing the cues it picks up. I believe that some people (for instance, global learners) may see and interpret the world in a more three-dimensional way. Letters, words, even lines of print seem to be viewed and analyzed from all angles — which makes steady, visual progression from one point to another very difficult to maintain. If this is true, it might account for the frequent reversals, both in reading and writing, and the slow fluency and loss of place that are so characteristic of this style of print-processing.

MISCUES AND MISCUE ANALYSIS

Miscue analysis is an approach to observing a person's reading behavior that takes into account all strategies for getting meaning from text.

The term "miscue" refers to the misreading of a word or phrase on a page. Such misreadings are not necessarily deemed errors. If the meaning of the text is preserved, the miscue is considered an efficient strategy. If meaning is lost, then the misreading is an error and indicates some sort of processing weakness.

High-quality miscues are those that don't resemble the text word but preserve meaning. Reading "That's a funny horse" when the text actually says "What a funny horse" is an example of a high-quality miscue. A poor-quality miscue is one that causes meaning loss. For example, reading "I'll the chicks ran into the house" when the text says "All the chicks ran into the house" shows that the reader is ignoring grammatical sense as well as meaning. Meaning is sacrificed in this case in favor of trying to accommodate the graphophonic display.

Close examination of at least 25 miscues is necessary to get a good picture of a reader's manner of dealing with print—which means using material hard enough that meaning will occasionally be lost and the reader will have to show his or her way of dealing with the situation. Below is an example of a miscue-coded passage, including definitions of the coding symbols used (Woods and Moe, p. 111a).

The sunlight shined into the mouth of the cave so

Mark could see/easily at first, but (the) farther he walked,
dark ©   ©   into this owner
the darker it grew. Boxer ran off to explore on his own.

Soon it grew so dark Mark could see nothing, but he

could hear water dripping off the cave walls. He touched
the   © could   lumpy
a wall with his hand to find it cold and damp. Mark began

to grow fearful, so he lit his candle and held it high to

look around.
                    he flamed
Suddenly, the flame went out. He heard a low growl
      © a   frightening
near him and saw a pair of fierce, green eyes glowing in
          turned   turn right
the dark! He tried to/relight the candle, but the first match
                                      © hold   * ©
went out! Finally, Mark's shaking hand held the lighted

candle high.
* 1. litten   2. held the light candle   3. lighted candle high

123

"Boxer!" he shouted. "Now I|^{crouched}recognize those green eyes of yours Let's get out of here!"

Here are the definitions of my coding system:

(AC) =	abandoned correct form	
(C) =	corrected	
Boxer ran ^{run} =	went back this far to correct	
(the) =	omitted circled word(s)	
walked =	repeated three times	
/// =	pause: one slash for each increment of time	
damp ^{lumpy} =	substitution	

Note: When I can't fit in a series of responses, I star the spot and write the sequence below or to the side.

For further information on miscue analysis, see Goodman and Burke (1972).

MORPHEME

A morpheme is the smallest unit of a letter-sound cluster that can still have a base of meaning:
- a single word, like *pan, sip* or *lake;*
- a "bound" morpheme, such as a prefix or suffix that carries a
- change of meaning in its application (*re-, ex-, -ing* or *-s,* for example);
  an orthographic root cluster such as *magi-,* the root for words like *magician, magical* and *imagination.*

ORAL CLOZE

Oral cloze ("cloze" is defined above) is leaving out words while reading aloud. When reading predictable texts, once I feel the children know the pattern I start leaving out words in the refrain, the second of a pair of rhyming words, or other words and phrases that can be easily predicted. Oral cloze encourages and strengthens prediction and confirmation strategies, reinforces use of the semantic and syntactic cueing systems, builds confidence, helps children learn new material and actively involves them in the reading.

PHONEMIC SEGMENTATION APPROACH

I use this term for approaches that teach reading as a decoding process in which each phoneme (letter-sound unit) is examined and articulated cumulatively to identify words. The graphophonic cueing system is thought to be the primary means of identifying words and to be rule-bound. Programs of this type describe sequences of skills the authors believe are logical, with reading material limited by the words and decoding rules previously taught. Some of these programs are so tightly structured that children who cannot master a particular skill cannot proceed to the next level.

PREDICTABLE TEXTS

Predictable texts are easy to read because they contain elements that provide concepts, language and structures either that are already familiar to readers or that make it possible for them to become quickly and easily memorable.

For emergent readers, texts with highly predictable rhyme schemes, strong rhythms, repeated refrains, exciting or humorous vocabulary and familiar or favorite topics make the best reading material. Such materials are quickly and easily remembered and support the transition from personal reconstruction of the text to the use of print. There is a wealth of material available now – so much, in fact, that we have to start being more careful about our selection. Some publishers are putting out "predictable" materials that have controlled vocabulary, poor illustrations and overpredictive elements (so repetitive as to be boring) or that promote dubious values. My rule of thumb is this: if it bothers me, it's likely to bother (or misinform) the children. There's too much to choose from to put up with poor literature.

For early readers, predictability moves away from the more immediately predictable elements, such as rhyme and single-line refrains, to material with predictable *structures,* such as folk and fairy tales and favorite character books (*Clifford, Curious*

George, Little Bear, Frog and Toad, etc.), where the actions and sequences are predictable. A book like Mercer Mayer's *What Do You Do with a Kangaroo?* is a good example of a transition text. It has a predictable, somewhat rhythmical structure and a repeated refrain, but without rhyme and with less predictable content elements.

Intermediate readers often become addicted to certain series (*Danny Dunn, Encyclopedia Brown, Nancy Drew,* etc.), books in which the characters, story structures and overall vocabularies remain essentially the same from book to book. Only the details of the plots change. The children who get hooked on these series are often the ones who become proficient readers, by virtue of sheer practice. During the two or three years they go through this phase, all other activities seem eclipsed by their reading. It's the time when they are driven fully into silent reading, perhaps in part because they discover they can find out "whodunit" much faster when they go into the silent mode.

PREDICTION AND CONFIRMATION STRATEGIES

Efficient readers rely on prediction or expectation as their key strategy. Prediction is like the fuel that keeps the car running; without fuel even the most expensive vehicle is useless.

We start making predictions the moment we pick up something to read. Even the type of material elicits expectations. A science magazine causes us to expect information, revelations, new discoveries and insights into matters related to physics, astronomy, biology, chemistry, perhaps even psychology. From a science fiction novel we expect adventure, perhaps mystery, often perspectives on human social dynamics in an unusual setting, and assuredly some imaginative manipulation of current scientific awareness. The sight of a newspaper will prepare us to receive the most up-to-date information on the state of the world.

Pictures, graphs, print size, book covers and any variety of other general aspects of appearance also cause us to anticipate what the text will tell us. For this reason it's important that the books used with beginning readers be of high quality, with pictures that complement the text so they can be used as clues for reading. The title is a vital cue. When we know what a story or poem is called, we can bring to bear our background knowledge and our memory of similar subjects, or perhaps other versions of the same piece of material, to help us read the piece.

Poetry, songs and stories with a predictable structure are the reading materials of choice for beginning readers because the tunes, rhyming patterns, predictable rhythms and repetition of lines or actions (as in folk tales) support them while they are developing strategies for dealing with print and building up an automatic sight-word bank they can use in various situations.

Once reading, we use the meaning we are already carrying from our expectations and from previously read material, plus our natural awareness of grammar to predict upcoming words. If the story is about a girl learning to ride a horse, it's unlikely we'll come across words like *octopus* or *Viking*. The brain narrows down possibilities almost instantaneously at the point any graphophonic sampling takes place and follows the sampling by a mental check to make sure everything still makes sense. This latter checking is the confirming part of the system. If all is well, prediction and sampling continue. If not, self-correction takes place, as described under Graphophonic Cueing System and Rerun.

For a more in-depth discussion refer to Goodman and Burke (1980).

READING LEVELS

This is a general term to indicate the difficulty level of material for a particular reader. First, traditional definitions:

* *Independent level:* material a person can read with 99% accuracy in word recognition and 90-100% accuracy in comprehension.
* *Instructional level:* material a person can read with 90-95% accuracy in word recognition (missing about one word in 20) and 70-90% accuracy in comprehension.
* *Frustration level:* anything below instructional.

However, it's important to define what is to be understood by terms like "word recognition" and "comprehension." If absolute accuracy in word recognition is required a reader is going to be considered poorer than if errors in word recognition are looked at through miscue analysis. Comprehension judged by answers to preset questions will be different from that assessed when readers are asked to give their recollection of the passage without the aid of prompting questions.

Another factor to note is that checking a number of longer passages gives a much clearer picture of the kind of material a reader can handle than limiting the assessment to one or two short passages. Interest, and therefore motivation and involvement, can play an important part in how well a person reads. Knowing a lot about horses will allow a reader to handle a difficult passage on that subject better than an easier passage on an unknown topic.

"Reading levels" are necessarily vague and imprecise and should be used only as general guides for choosing reading material or placing readers for instruction.

RECONSTRUCTION OF TEXT

Children in the emergent reader stage are often said to be memorizing stories. The term "memorize" can be misleading, however. It does not mean a dog-training kind of rote recitation devoid of volition, personal interpretation and variations in vocabulary choice based on the child's oral language experiences, all of which do come into play during this stage. Although memorization is involved, the process is more complex than that.

Children ask for favorite stories over and over, and in the process of hearing and practicing on their own, they memorize major chunks of the author's language. But they are also quite content to make their own choices of words and phrases, to omit parts that to them are insignificant, and even to create whole episodes from their own store of experience and imagining. What they are doing is less of a memorization task and more of a re-creation or reconstruction of the story, in their own terms. As they gradually become more aware of the fixed nature of written texts, their reconstructions come closer and closer to the author's actual words, but even mature readers "create" parts of texts as they read. When I make a meaningful substitution and don't bother to self-correct, or when I skip a portion of text because I think I'm already familiar with the ideas it contains, I'm replacing the author's construct with my own.

RERUN

Rerun, or repetition, is a strategy readers use to re-establish the meaning or grammatical sense when they've had to stop moving ahead for some reason. Even the most highly efficient readers use it. For example, an unexpected piece of information may require the rereading of a previous piece of text to double-check something first judged insignificant. Meaning-oriented readers who are unsure of themselves overuse this strategy because they stop themselves so frequently. Generally, however, it is used in a balanced way as part of the prediction/sampling/self-correction cycle.

SEMANTIC CUEING SYSTEM

The semantic cueing system is the first and most important system that comes into play in the reading process. Although all three cueing systems are interdependent, without this one, reading is merely word-calling.

"Semantic" refers to meaning. When people say, "It's a matter of semantics," they are saying it's a question of the interpretation of the meaning of the words under discussion. When we use language we expect it to make sense. As we read we predict that what is coming will make sense, and we are constantly testing the intake against personal concepts of what's logical, sensible and meaningful. For reading to be meaningful, the reader must have sufficient background knowledge to make connections with the author's message. As an example, I was recently trying to read a book on archetypes in mythology, and although I could identify every word in the book, I was almost totally lost because I didn't have sufficient background in Jungian psychology to connect with the author's discussions.

Children who have been led to believe that reading is defined as word identification often don't use the semantic cueing system. Their reading is characterized by "grunt and groan" sounding out of words, patchy fluency and poor comprehension.

SIGHT-WORD BANK

This is the collection of words a reader can recognize automatically, with no hesitation and without the use of word-attack skills. The larger a sight-word bank, the more context readers will have with which to surround unknown or partially familiar words. The more context there is, the easier it is to figure out what will fit meaningfully at a particular spot in the text. It's important, therefore, that a beginning reader acquire a large and solid base of sight words. Natural readers (those who read before coming to school) acquire this base by matching their memory of favorite stories and poems back to the print on the page so many times that eventually they remember the individual words when they see them in other situations.

SKILLS

I use "skills" to refer to the specific tools used in narrowly defined reading situations. Using a rule like the "two vowels" rule or the "magic e" rule is a skill. I think of blending, using initial consonants for cues, making word-family associations and syllabification as skills. Skills are helpful tools, but limited in scope.

STRATEGIES

To me a strategy is a general plan of action used in the reading process, one that can be applied in any reading situation to help create meaning from text: predicting, self-correcting, reading ahead, rerunning—and even more general actions like rejecting a book that's too difficult or too boring—are strategies. Unlike skills, strategies aren't dependent on a particular graphic display or set of circumstances to be effective.

SUBVOCALIZE

I use "subvocalize" to mean reading below speech level, even completely silently, but still controlled by word-by-word reading in terms of eye flow and fluency. That is, the reader finds it necessary to focus on each word individually and pronounce it to himself rather than take in phrase chunks, which allows for more fluid reading. An observer may see the reader whispering, mouthing or merely moving facial muscles. Or there may be no lower face movement at all, but the eyes can be seen to stop and focus individually on each word. My definition may not be the common one.

TEXT

I mean *any* piece of written material: a sign, a cereal box, a form, a dictionary entry, a telephone book entry, an advertisement, as well as the more commonly envisioned types of text: stories, songs, poems, information pieces, etc.

VOICE-MATCHING

This term refers to word-by-word matching during oral reading. When children move from the emergent to the early reader stage they begin to use the printed text itself to guide their reading. They begin pointing to the words in the manner they've seen modeled and start to recognize some words on sight. They can voice-match when they are able to read a previously memorized story, accurately pointing to each word unit as they proceed orally, although they don't necessarily know the words in isolation. The breakthrough comes when they discover that some words are multi-syllabic and they have to hold their finger longer under those words. Some children can syllable-point fairly early. Others just use timing to match the speed of their finger with the oral utterance.

Bibliography

Allen, P. David and Dorothy Watson. *Findings of Research in Miscue Analysis: Classroom Implications*. Urbana, Ill: ERIC, 1976.

Alper, Joseph. "Our Dual Memory" in *Science 86,* July/August, 1986, pp. 44-49.

Ashton-Warner, Sylvia. *Teacher.* New York: Bantam Books, 1963.

Associated Press. "Brain, immune system found to speak common language" in *The Recorder.* Greenfield, Mass, May 12, 1987.

Associated Press. "Researchers find way to help some dyslexics" in *The Recorder.* Greenfield, Mass, May 14, 1987.

Baskwill, Jane and Paulette Whitman. *A Guide to Classroom Publishing.* Richmond Hill, Ont: Scholastic-TAB Publications, 1986.

Baskwill, Jane and Paulette Whitman. *Moving On: a Whole Language Sourcebook for Grades Three and Four.* Richmond Hill, Ont: Scholastic-TAB Publications, 1988.

Baskwill, Jane and Paulette Whitman. *Whole Language Sourcebook.* Richmond Hill, Ont: Scholastic-TAB Publications, 1986.

Blakeslee, Thomas R. *The Right Brain: A New Understanding of the Unconscious Mind and Its Creative Powers.* New York: Berkley Books, 1983.

Bolton, Faye et al. *Teacher's Resource Book: Bookshelf Stage 1.* (Also for Stages 2 through 7.) Sydney: Horwitz Grahame Books Pty Ltd, 1986. Distributed in the U.S. by Scholastic Inc, in Canada by Scholastic-TAB Publications, in Australia and New Zealand by Ashton Scholastic.

Butler, Andrea. *The Story Box in the Classroom: Stage 1.* (Also for Stages 2-7.) Melbourne: Rigby Educational, 1984. Distributed by the Wright Group.

Calkins, Lucy McCormick. *The Art of Teaching Writing.* Portsmouth, NH: Heinemann Educational Books, 1986.

Calkins, Lucy McCormick. *Lessons from a Child.* Portsmouth, NH: Heinemann Educational Books, 1983.

Carbo, Marie. "Advanced Book Recording: Turning It Around for Poor Readers" in *Early Years/K-8,* January, 1985, pp. 46-48.

Carbo, Marie. "Recorded Books = Remarkable Reading Gains" in *Early Years/K-8,* November, 1984, pp. 44-47.

Cochrane, Orin. *The Great Gray Owl.* Winnipeg: Whole Language Consultants, 1986.

Courtney, Rosemary et al. "Don't Hold Your Breath" in *Evaluation Resource Book for Hockey Cards and Hopscotch.* Don Mills, Ont: Thomas Nelson (Canada), 1980.

Courtney, Rosemary et al. "The Monster of Blue Lake" in *Evaluation Resource Book for Grade One.* Don Mills, Ont: Thomas Nelson (Canada), 1980.

Courtney, Rosemary et al. "Whiplash Escapes" in *Evaluation Resource Book for Grade Two.* Don Mills, Ont: Thomas Nelson (Canada), 1980.

Doake, David B. "Reading: A Language Learning Activity." Address presented at the University of Victoria International Reading Research Seminar on Linguistic Awareness and Learning to Read, Victoria, BC, June 26-30, 1979.

Doake, David B. *Reading Begins at Birth.* Richmond Hill, Ont: Scholastic-TAB Publications, 1988.

Duane, Drake D. "Summary of Current Research Into Dyslexia." Address given at the Fourteenth Annual Conference of the New York Branch of the Orton Dyslexia Society, March 13, 1987.

Durden-Smith, Jo. "Male and Female Why?" in *Quest/80,* October, 1980, pp. 15-19.

"Enzymes that help you think" in *Science Digest.* July, 1982. p. 92.

Fischman, Joshua. "Mapping the Mind" in *Psychology Today,* September, 1985.

Goodman, Kenneth S. "Manifesto for a Reading Revolution" in *Claremont Reading Conference Yearbook,* vol. 40. Claremont, CA, 1976, pp. 16-28.

Goodman, Ken. *What's Whole in Whole Language?* Richmond Hill, Ont: Scholastic-TAB Publications, 1986. Published in the U.S. by Heinemann Educational Books.

Goodman, Yetta M. and Carolyn L. Burke. *Reading Miscue Inventory Manual: Procedure for Diagnosis and Evaluation.* New York: Macmillan, 1972.

Goodman, Yetta M. and Carolyn Burke. *Reading Strategies: Focus on Comprehension.* New York: Holt, Rinehart and Winston, 1980.

Grahame, Kenneth. *The Wind in the Willows.* New York: Charles Scribner Sons, 1960, p. 80.

Graves, Donald H. *Writing: Teachers and Children at Work.* Portsmouth, NH: Heinemann Educational Books, 1983.

Hancock, Joelie and Susan Hill. *Literature-based reading programs at work.* Melbourne: Australian Reading Association, 1987.

Harste, Jerome C., Virginia A. Woodward and Carolyn L. Burke. *Language Stories and Literacy Lessons.* Portsmouth, NH: Heinemann Educational Books, 1984.

Holdaway, Don. *The Foundations of Literacy.* Sydney: Ashton Scholastic, 1979. Distributed in the U.S. by Heinemann Educational Books.

Holdaway, Don. *Independence in Reading.* Sydney: Ashton Scholastic, 1980.

Holdaway, Don. *Stability and Change in Literacy Learning.* Portsmouth, NH: Heinemann Educational Books, 1984.

Hornsby, David and Deborah Sukarna, with Jo-Ann Parry. *Read On: A Conference Approach to Reading.* Sydney: Horwitz Grahame Books Pty Ltd, 1986.

Horton, Elizabeth. "Spatial Hormones" in *Science Digest,* January, 1983, p. 62.

Itskoff, Seymour. *How We Learn to Read.* Ashfield, MA: Press, 1985.

Jewell, Margaret Greer and Miles V. Zintz. *Learning to Read Naturally.* Dubuque, Iowa: Kendall/Hunt Publishing, 1986.

Johnstone, J. et al. "Regional Brain Activity in Dyslexic and Control Children during Reading Tasks: Visual Probe Event-Related Potentials" in *Brain and Language,* March, 1984, pp. 223-254.

Lipa, Sally E. "Reading Disability: A New Look at an Old Issue" in *Journal of Learning Disabilities,* October, 1983, pp. 453-457.

Manzo, Anthony V. "The ReQuest Procedure" in *Journal of Reading,* November, 1969, pp. 123-126.

Masland, Richard L. "What is Dyslexia." Address given at the Fourteenth Annual Conference of The New York Branch of the Orton Dyslexia Society, March 12, 1987.

Mayer, Mercer. *What Do You Do With a Kangaroo?* Auckland: Ashton Scholastic, 1980.

Melser, June. *The Story Box: Teacher's Book*. Auckland: Shortland Publications, 1983. Distributed by the Wright Group.

Newkirk, Thomas and Nancie Atwell, eds. *Understanding Writing*. Chelmsford, Mass: The Northeast Regional Exchange, Inc, 1982.

Pavlidis, George T. "Eye Movements in Dyslexia: Their Diagnostic Significance" in *Journal of Learning Disabilities*, January, 1985, pp. 42-50.

Restak, Richard M. *The Brain: The Last Frontier*. New York: Warner Books, 1979.

Rico, Gabrielle Lusser. *Writing the Natural Way*. Los Angeles: J.P. Tarcher, 1983.

Rosenfield, Israel. "A Hero of the Brain" in *New York Times Review of Books*, November 21, 1985, pp. 49-52.

Smith, Frank. *Understanding Reading*. New York: Holt, Rinehart and Winston, 1982.

Smith, Shelley D. "Genetics of Dyslexia: Progress in Identifying Single Genes." Address given at the Fourteenth Annual Conference of the Orton Dyslexia Society, March 12, 1987.

Turbill, Jan, ed. *No Better Way to Teach Writing*. Rosebery, NSW: Primary English Teaching Association, 1982. Distributed in the U.S. by Heinemann Educational Books.

Vellutino, Frank R. and Donna M. Scanlon. "Experimental Evidence for the Effects of Instructional Bias on Word Identification" in *Exceptional Children*, October, 1986, pp. 145-155.

Williams, Linda Verlee. *Teaching for the Two-sided Mind*. Englewood Cliffs, NJ: Prentice-Hall, 1983.

Woods, Mary Lynn and Alden J. Moe. *Analytical Reading Inventory*. Columbus, OH: Charles Merrill, 1977.

Index